Show me

Word® for Windows™ 6

A Visual Guide to the Basics

Peter Aitken, revised by Sherry Kinkoph

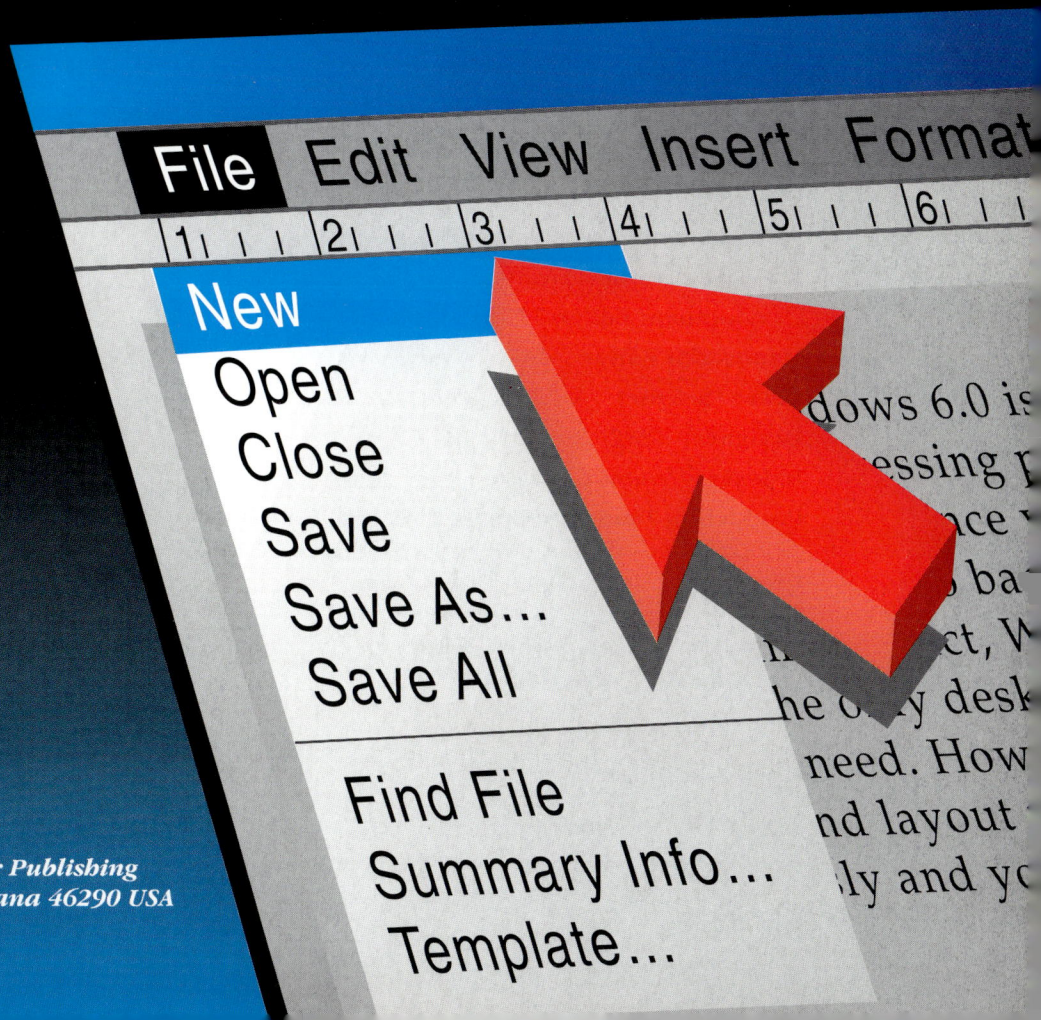

alpha
books

A Division of Prentice Hall Computer Publishing
1 W. 103rd Street, Indianapolis, Indiana 46290 USA

© 1993 Alpha Books

International Standard Book Number:1-56761-347-0
Library of Congress Catalog Card Number: 93-71737

95 94 93   8 7 6 5 4 3 2 1

Interpretation of the printing code: the rightmost number of the first series of numbers is the year of the book's printing; the rightmost number of the second series of numbers is the number of the book's printing. For example, a printing code of 93-1 shows that the first printing of the book occurred in 1993.

Screen reproductions in this book were created by means of the program Collage Plus from Inner Media, Inc., Hollis, NH.

Printed in the United States of America

Publisher   *Marie Butler-Knight*

Associate Publisher   *Lisa A. Bucki*

Managing Editor   *Elizabeth Keaffaber*

Development Editor   *Faithe Wempen*

Manuscript Editor   *Audra Gable*

Cover Designer   *Scott Fullmer*

Designer   *Roger Morgan*

Indexer   *Jeanne Clark*

Production Team   *Diana Bigham, Katy Bodenmiller, Brad Chinn, Scott Cook, Tim Cox, Meshell Dinn, Mark Enochs, Howard Jones, Beth Rago, Carrie Roth, Greg Simsic, Marc Shecter*

Special thanks to C. Herbert Feltner for ensuring the technical accuracy of this book.

CONTENTS

INTRODUCTION

Have you ever said to yourself, "I wish someone would just show me how to use Word for Windows." If you have, this Show Me book is for you. In it, you won't find detailed explanations of what's going on in your computer each time you enter a command. Instead, you will see pictures that show you, step by step, how to perform a particular task.

This book will make you feel as though you have your very own personal trainer standing next to you, pointing at the screen and showing you exactly what to do.

WHAT IS MICROSOFT WORD FOR WINDOWS 6.0?

So what exactly is Word for Windows 6.0? It is a word processing program designed to be used for creating, editing, and printing documents. A document can be anything that contains words: a half-page memo, a 10-page report, or a 500-page book.

Most of the time, we'll just call the product Word rather than using the full name "Microsoft Word for Windows." Since Word is a Windows-based product, it's designed to be used from within another program, Microsoft Windows. If you're not familiar with Windows, don't worry—this book will ease you into it. (There is another version of Word, Word for DOS 5.5, that is not Windows-based, but we're not going to cover it in this book.)

If you haven't worked with a word processor in several years, be prepared for some big surprises. Word processors such as Word for Windows 6.0 come with a huge assortment of features to dress up your documents. In addition to the basics of entering text, making corrections, and printing, you can

- Change the letters and spacing to create professional-looking documents.

- Automatically check spelling and correct mistakes.

- Use headers, footers, footnotes, and page numbers, all automatically generated.

- Include pictures in your documents.

- Work on more than one document at the same time.

- Display information in tables.

- Preview and fine-tune your page before you print it.

What Does Word Look Like?

Word looks a lot like other Windows-based programs you may have seen. (If you haven't seen a Windows-based program before, that's okay.) The main screen is a rectangular window. The text you type appears in the middle, and around the edges are buttons, menus, borders, and other items that help you control Word.

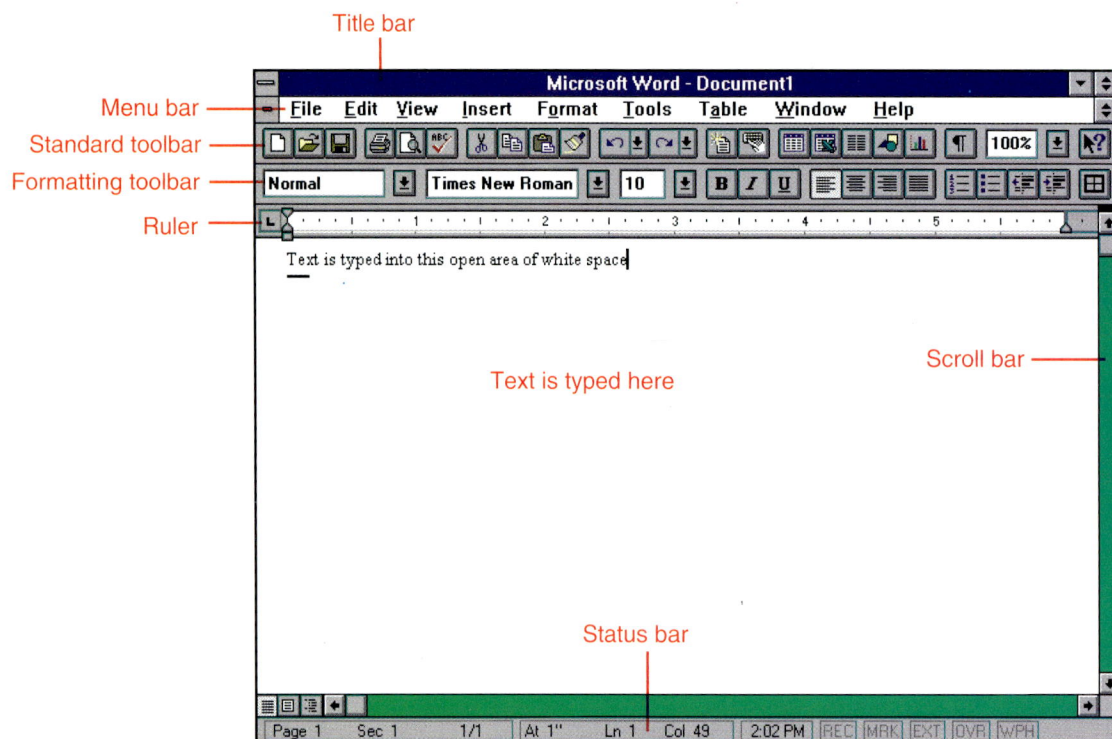

Title bar

Menu bar ——

Standard toolbar ——

Formatting toolbar ——

Ruler ——

Microsoft Word - Document1

File   Edit   View   Insert   Format   Tools   Table   Window   Help

Normal   Times New Roman   10   B I U

Text is typed into this open area of white space

Scroll bar ——

Text is typed here

Status bar

Page 1   Sec 1   1/1   At 1"   Ln 1   Col 49   2:02 PM   REC MRK EXT OVR WPH

Don't worry about memorizing the parts of the window now; you'll learn more about them later in the book.

HOW TO USE THIS BOOK

Using this book is as simple as falling off your chair. Just flip to the task that you want to perform and follow the steps. You will see easy step-by-step instructions that tell you which keys to press and which commands to select. You will also see step-by-step pictures that show you what to do. Follow the steps or the pictures (or both) to complete the task. Here's an example of a set of instructions from this book.

Saving a Document

1 Click on **File** or press **Alt+F**.

2 Click on Save **As** or press **A**.

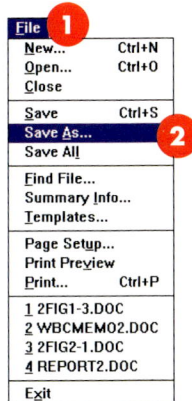

3 Enter the document name in the File **N**ame box.

4 If desired, select drive, directory, and file type options.

5 Click **OK** or press **Enter**.

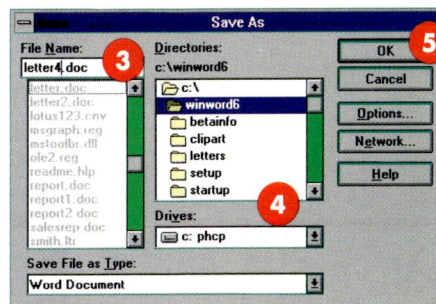

Every computer book has its own way of telling you which buttons to push and which keys to press. Here's how this book handles those formalities:

- Keys that you should press appear as they do on your keyboard (for example, press **Alt** or press **F10**). If you need to press more than one key at once, the keys are separated with plus signs. For example, if the text tells you to press **Alt+F**, hold down the **Alt** key and press the **F** key.

- Text that you should type is printed in **boldface type like this**.

- Some features are activated by selecting a menu and then a command. If I tell you to "select **F**ile **N**ew," you should open the **File** menu and select the **New** command. In this book, the selection letter is printed in boldface for easy recognition.

3

Definitions in Plain English

In addition to the basic step-by-step approach, pages may contain Learning the Lingo definitions to help you understand key terms. These definitions are placed off to the side, so you can easily skip them.

LEARNING THE LINGO

Pull-down menu: A menu that appears at the top of the screen, listing various commands. The menu is not visible until you select it from the menu bar. The menu then drops down, covering a small part of the screen.

Quick Refreshers

If you need to know how to perform some other task in order to perform the current task, look for a Quick Refresher. With the Quick Refresher, you won't have to flip through the book to learn how to perform the other task; the information is right where you need it.

QUICK REFRESHER

Making dialog box selections

List box. Click on a list item to choose it. Use the scroll bar to view additional items.

Drop-down list. Click on the down arrow to the right of the list to display it. Click on the desired item.

Text box. Click to place the I-beam in the box. Type your entry.

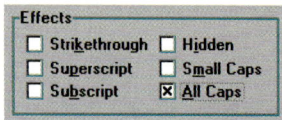

Check box. Click on a box to select or deselect it. (You can select more than one.)

Tips, Ideas, and Shortcuts

Throughout this book, you will encounter tips that provide important information about a task or tell you how to perform the task more quickly.

TIP

Keyboard Shortcuts Here are some keyboard shortcuts for working Word for Windows:

Open a document	**CTRL** + **F 12**	Copy	**CTRL** + **C**
Save a document	**SHIFT** + **F 12**	Paste	**CTRL** + **V**
Print a document	**CTRL** + **SHIFT** + **F 12**	Go To	**F5**
Cut	**CTRL** + **X**	Exit Word	**ALT** + **F4**

Exercises

Because most people learn by doing, several exercises throughout the book give you additional practice performing a task.

Practice using the Zoom feature by following these steps:

1 Click on **V**iew or press **Alt+V**.

2 Click on **Z**oom or press **Z**.

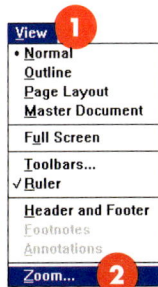

3 Select the zoom percentage you wish to view the document in.

4 Check the preview window to see a sample of zoom size.

5 Click **OK** or press **Enter**.

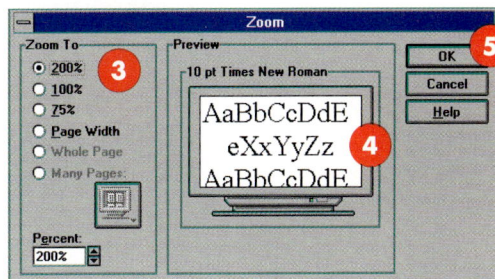

5

Introduction

Where Should You Start?

If this is your first encounter with computers, read the next section, "Quick Computer Tour," before reading anything else. This section explains some computer basics that you need to know in order to get your computer up and running.

Once you know the basics, you can work through this book from beginning to end or skip around from task to task, as needed. If you decide to skip around, there are several ways you can find what you're looking for:

• Use the Table of Contents at the front of this book to find a specific task you want to perform.

• Use the complete index at the back of this book to look up a specific task or topic and find the page number on which it is covered.

• Use the color-coded sections to find groups of related tasks.

• Flip through the book and look at the task titles at the top of the pages. This method works best if you know the general location of the task in the book.

QUICK COMPUTER TOUR

If this is your first time in front of a computer, the next few sections will teach you the least you need to know to get started.

Parts of a Computer

Think of a computer as a car. The system unit holds the engine that powers the computer. The monitor is like the windshield that lets you see where you're going. And the keyboard and mouse are like the steering wheel, which allow you to control the computer.

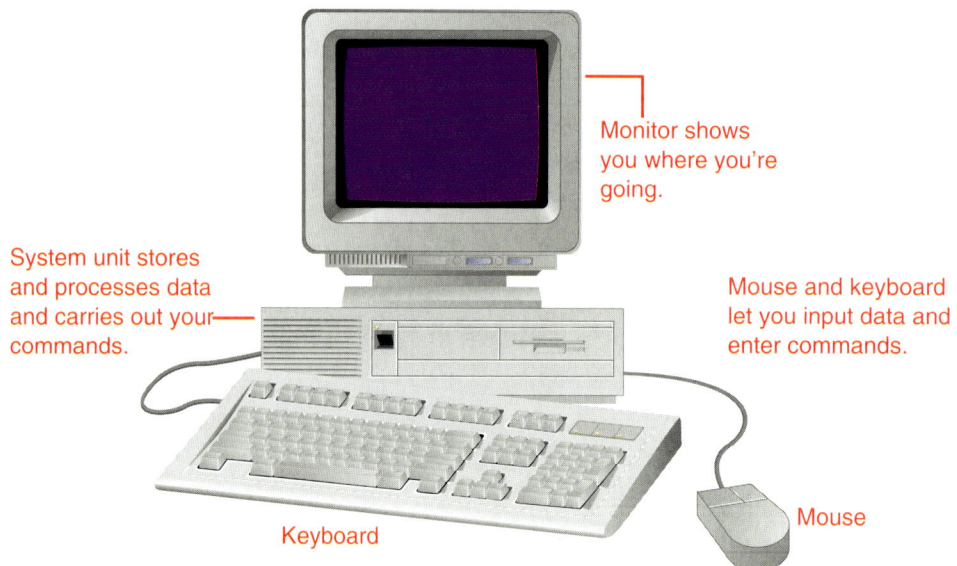

Monitor shows you where you're going.

System unit stores and processes data and carries out your commands.

Mouse and keyboard let you input data and enter commands.

Keyboard

Mouse

The System Unit

The system unit contains three basic elements: a central processing unit (CPU), which does all the "thinking" for the computer; random-access memory (RAM), which stores instructions and data while the CPU is processing it; and disk drives, which store information permanently on disks to keep the information safe. It also contains several ports (at the back), which allow you to connect other devices to it, such as a keyboard, mouse, and printer.

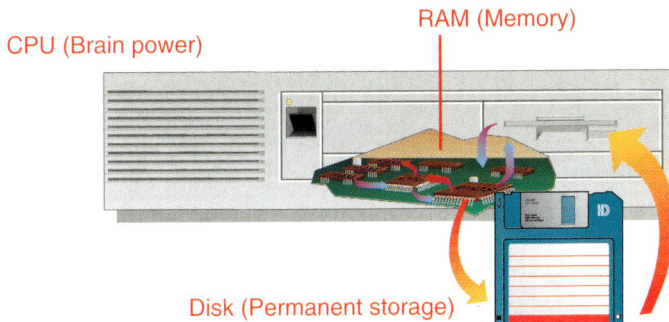

CPU (Brain power)

RAM (Memory)

Disk (Permanent storage)

Using a Keyboard

The keyboard is no mystery. It contains a set of alphanumeric (letter and number) keys for entering text, arrow keys for moving around on-screen, and function keys (F1, F2, and so on) for entering commands. It also has some odd keys, including Alt (Alternative), Ctrl (Control), and Esc (Escape) that perform special actions.

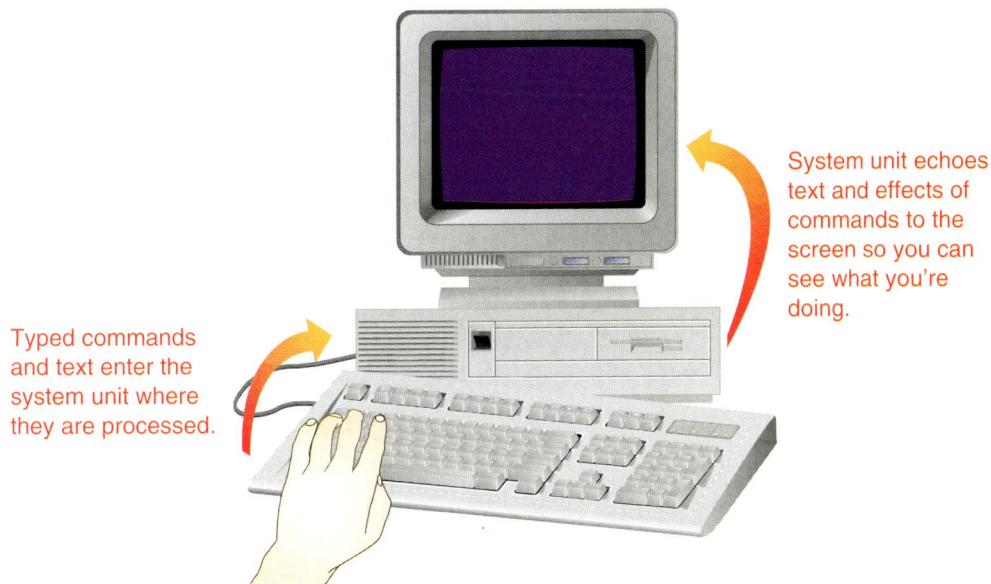

Typed commands and text enter the system unit where they are processed.

System unit echoes text and effects of commands to the screen so you can see what you're doing.

Using a Mouse

Like the keyboard, a mouse allows you to communicate with the computer. You roll the mouse around on your desk to move a mouse pointer on the screen. You can use the pointer to open menus and select other items on-screen. Here are some mouse techniques you must master:

Pointing. To point, roll the mouse on your desk until the tip of the mouse pointer is on the item to which you want to point.

Clicking. To click on an item, point to the desired item, and then hold the mouse steady while you press and release the mouse button. Use the left mouse button unless I tell you specifically to use the right button.

Double-clicking. To double-click, hold the mouse steady while you press and release the mouse button twice quickly.

Right-clicking. To right-click, click using the right mouse button instead of the left button.

Drag. To drag, hold down the left mouse button and move the mouse to a new position.

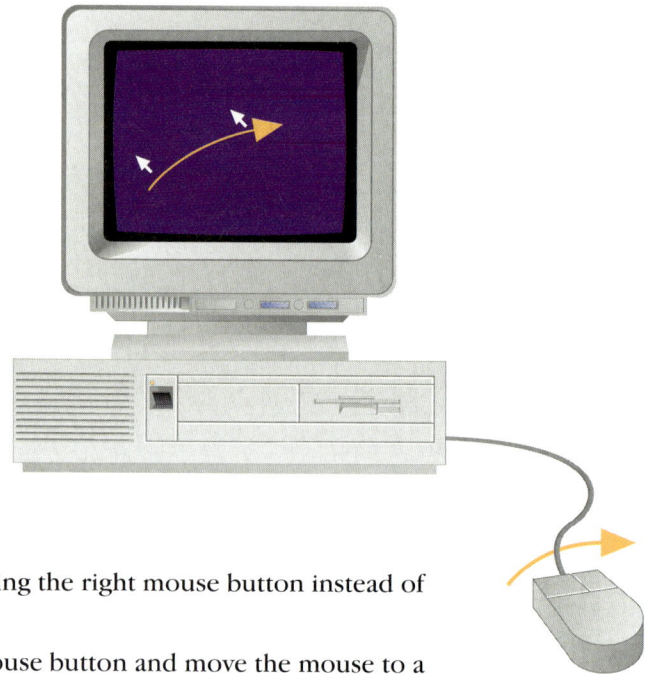

Understanding Disks, Directories, and Files

Whatever you type (a letter, a list of names, a tax return) is stored only in your computer's temporary memory and is erased when the electricity is turned off. To protect your work, you must save it in a file on a disk.

A file is like a folder that you might use to store a report or a letter. You name the file so that you can later find and retrieve the information it contains.

Save whatever you type in a named file.

REPORT

Files are stored on disks. Your computer probably has a hard disk inside it (called drive C) to which you can save your files. You can also save files to floppy disks, which you insert into the slots (the floppy disk drives) on the front of the computer.

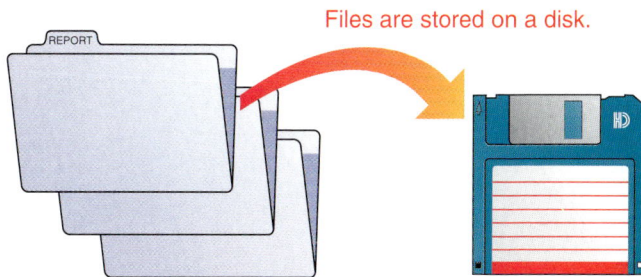

Files are stored on a disk.

REPORT

To keep files organized on a disk, you can create directories on the disk. Each directory acts as a drawer in a filing cabinet, storing a group of related files. Although you can create directories on both floppy and hard disks, most people use directories only on hard disks.

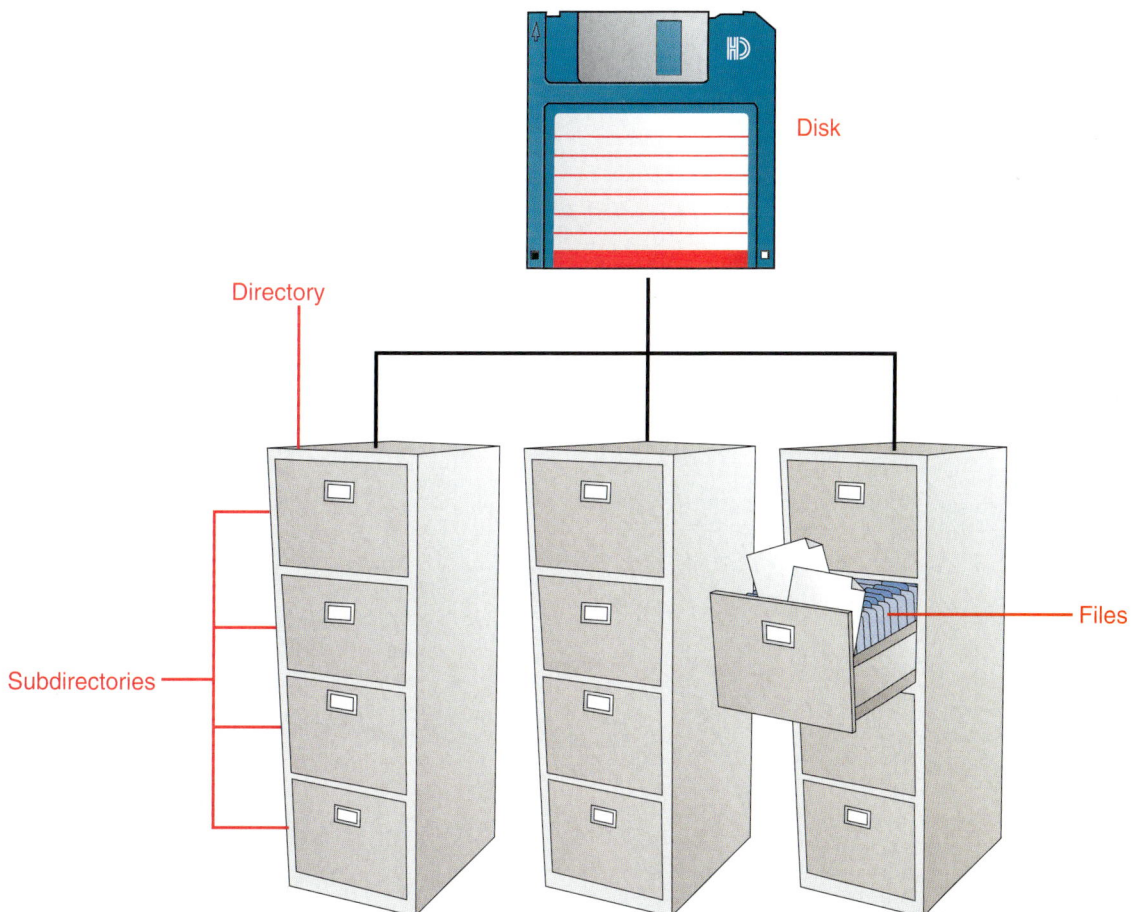

Disk

Directory

Subdirectories

Files

PART 1

Basic Word Tasks

Before you can run, you have to spend some time walking. In this section you will learn the most basic Word for Windows tasks—starting the program, how to use menus and dialog boxes, and so on. Because so many of the more advanced features use these basic procedures as building blocks, you'll be glad later that you took the time to master them now.

- Starting Windows
- Starting Word
- Understanding the Word Screen
- Using Word Menus
- Working with Dialog Boxes
- Working with the Standard Toolbar
- Working with the Formatting Toolbar
- Getting Help from Word
- Exiting Word

STARTING WINDOWS

When to Start Windows

You must start Windows before you can use Word for Windows 6.0. Starting Windows displays the Windows *desktop* on your screen. You'll see the Program Manager, which you use to run other *applications* (such as Word).

Starting Windows

1 Make sure your computer and monitor are turned on. Then at the *DOS prompt* (which looks like **C:>** or **C:\>**), type **win**.

2 Press **Enter**.

```
C:\>win
```
1

ENTER **2**

LEARNING THE LINGO

DOS Prompt: A set of characters on the left side of the screen when you first turn on your computer, followed by a blinking underline. DOS commands are typed in at the DOS prompt.

Applications: Programs that run on your computer, such as word processing, spreadsheet, database, and graphics programs.

When to Start Word

Before you can use Word for Windows 6.0 to create or edit a document, you must start (run) it. This loads the program and displays it on your screen.

To start a program you use the Windows Program Manager screen, which is displayed when you start Windows. You need to locate the Microsoft Applications *icon*, a small graphical symbol with the label "Microsoft Applications" below it. This icon represents the Microsoft Applications program group. Once it's opened, you'll see the Microsoft Applications program group window.

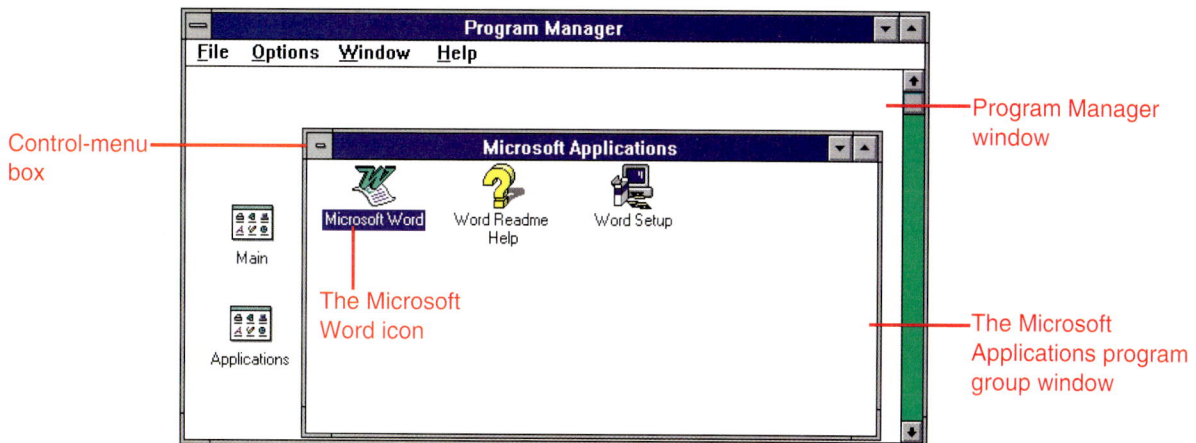

Control-menu box

Program Manager window

The Microsoft Word icon

The Microsoft Applications program group window

LEARNING THE LINGO

Icon: A small picture on the screen that represents a program, an action you can take, or a piece of information.

Highlight: A solid color bar or outline around an icon or menu command that indicates you have selected it.

Document: Work, such as a letter or a memo, created using a word processing program.

TIP

How Do You Open the Program Manager? If the Microsoft Applications program group is not open, it appears at the bottom of the Program Manager window as an icon. You need to open the Program Manager window in order to start Word (as described in this task). To open it, double-click on the icon, or press **Ctrl+Tab** until the icon is highlighted. Then press **Enter** to open the program group.

Basic Word Tasks

STARTING WORD

Starting Word for Windows

1 Double-click on the Microsoft Office program group icon, or press **Ctrl+Tab** until the icon is highlighted and then press **Enter**.

2 Double-click on the Microsoft Word icon, or press the arrow keys until the Microsoft Word icon is highlighted and then press **Enter**.

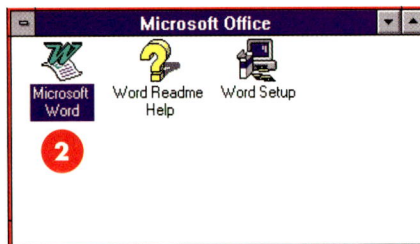

QUICK REFRESHER

As you learned in the Introduction, you can use the mouse to point and select items on-screen. Here are the mouse techniques you will need to use in this section:

Point: To move your mouse so that the arrow on-screen is directly over the item you want to select.

Click: To press the left mouse button while holding the mouse pointer steadily over the item to be selected.

Double-click: To quickly press the left mouse button twice in rapid succession.

TIP

Different Icons? The icons displayed on your Program Manager screen depend on the programs that are installed on your computer. Your screens will probably not look exactly the same as the ones shown in this book.

TIP

Closing the Microsoft Office Program Group Window After you've exited the Word program (explained in the task "Exiting Word for Windows" later in this section), you'll be returned to the Microsoft Office program group window. To close the window, double-click the Control-menu box, or press **Alt+F4**.

UNDERSTANDING THE WORD SCREEN

What Are the Parts of the Word Screen?

When you start Word for Windows, it displays the screen shown in the figure below. Each part of the screen has a name and a specific purpose. It's a good idea to familiarize yourself with the screen before you begin the tasks in Part 2.

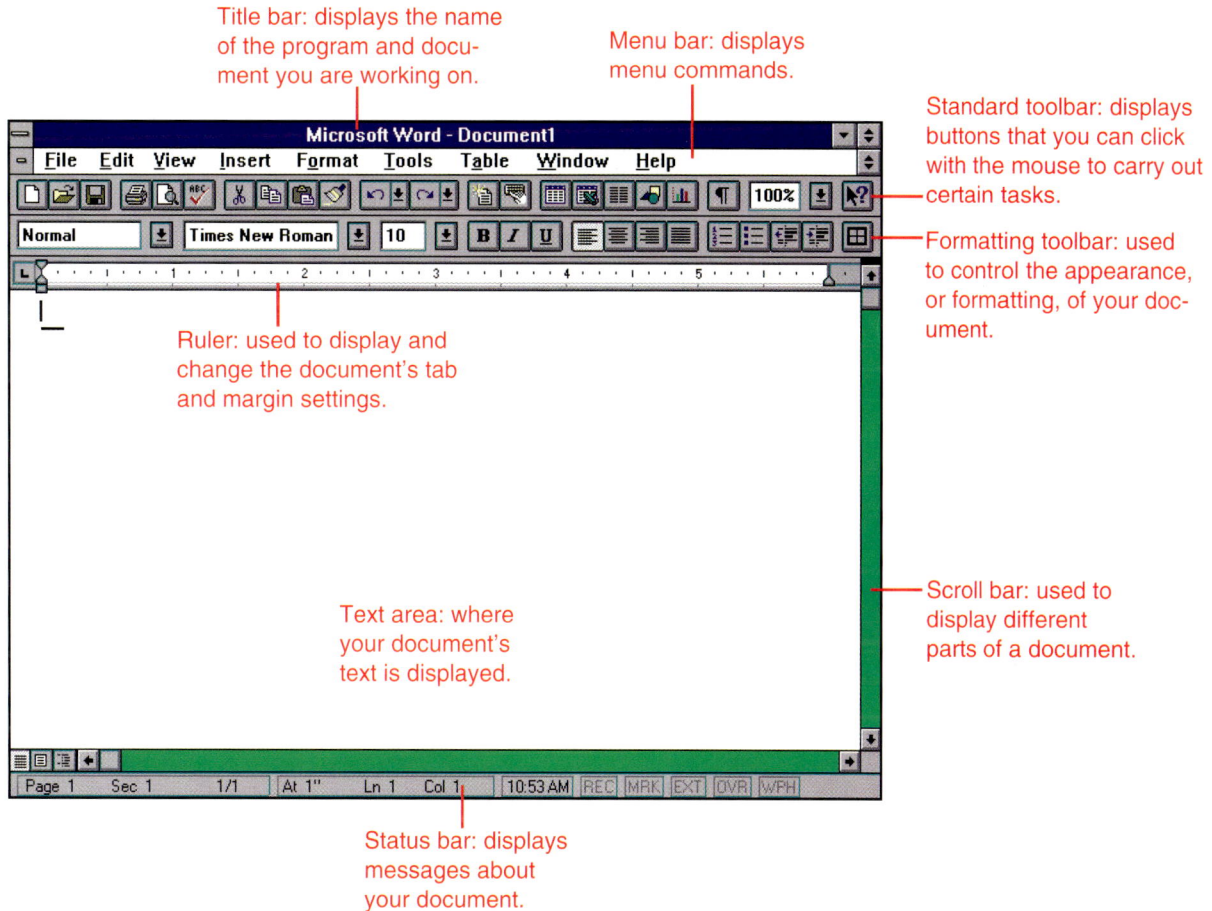

Title bar: displays the name of the program and document you are working on.

Menu bar: displays menu commands.

Standard toolbar: displays buttons that you can click with the mouse to carry out certain tasks.

Formatting toolbar: used to control the appearance, or formatting, of your document.

Ruler: used to display and change the document's tab and margin settings.

Text area: where your document's text is displayed.

Scroll bar: used to display different parts of a document.

Status bar: displays messages about your document.

LEARNING THE LINGO

Commands: Orders that tell the computer what to do.

Formatting: Changing the look of text, such as making it bolder or larger, or changing its positioning. Also called *attributes* or *text enhancements*.

USING WORD MENUS

What Are Menus?

You use *menus* to issue commands to Word for Windows, telling it what you want it to do. Menus offer lists of commands to choose from. You'll find the menu names displayed on the menu bar on your screen.

To use Word menus and commands, you must first open the menu and then select the command of your choice. When you open a menu, it drops down to reveal a list of commands like those shown in the figure below. You can use the mouse or the keyboard to select menu commands. Notice that each menu name and command has an underlined letter. This is called the *selection letter*. If you're using the keyboard to select a menu from the menu bar, you can hold down the **Alt** key and press the underlined selection letter to reveal the menu. When a menu list is revealed, you can choose commands from the list by typing the corresponding selection letter. If you're using the mouse, point to the menu name or the menu item you want to select and click the left mouse button.

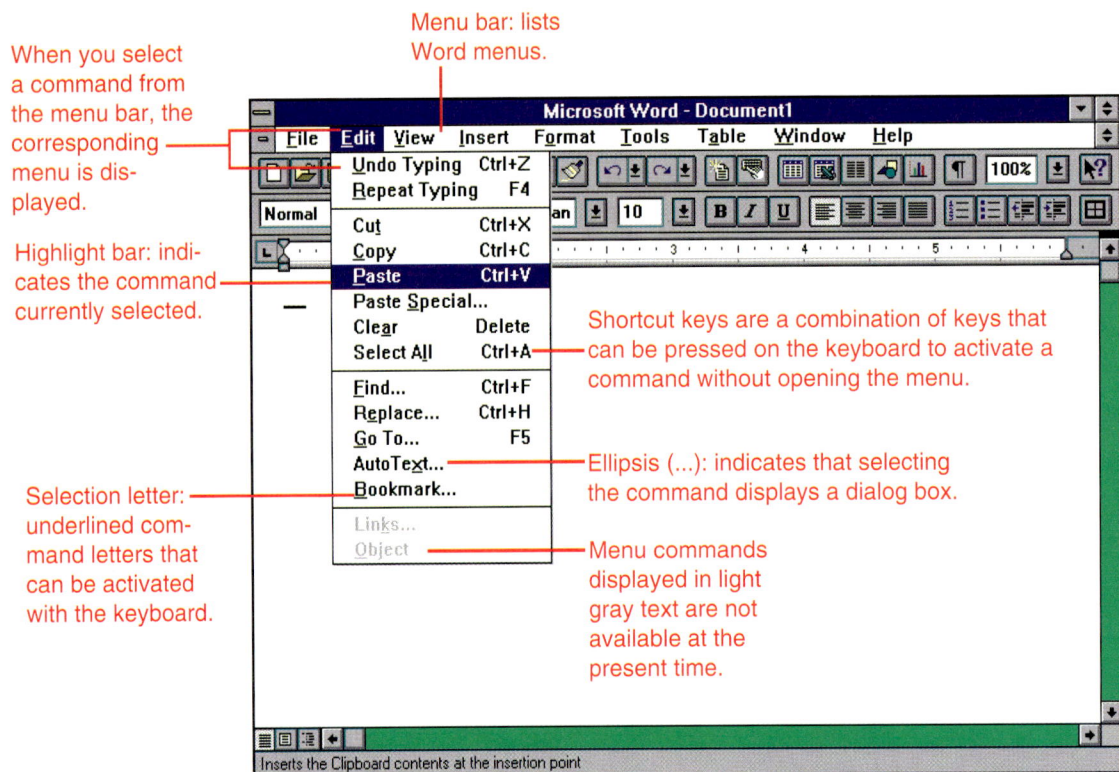

Menu bar: lists Word menus.

When you select a command from the menu bar, the corresponding menu is displayed.

Highlight bar: indicates the command currently selected.

Selection letter: underlined command letters that can be activated with the keyboard.

Shortcut keys are a combination of keys that can be pressed on the keyboard to activate a command without opening the menu.

Ellipsis (...): indicates that selecting the command displays a dialog box.

Menu commands displayed in light gray text are not available at the present time.

Selecting Menu Commands

1 Click on the menu name on the menu bar, or hold down the **Alt** key and then press the underlined letter in the menu name.

2 Click on the command name, or press the underlined letter in the command name.

File	1
New...	Ctrl+N
Open...	Ctrl+O
Close	
Save	**Ctrl+S**
Save As...	
Save All	
Find File...	
Summary Info...	
Templates...	
Page Setup...	
Print Preview	
Print...	Ctrl+P
1 ASSIMILI.DOC	
2 ARTICLES.DOC	
3 COMPLNT.DOC	
4 INVOICE1.DOC	
Exit	

LEARNING THE LINGO

Shortcut key: A key, or combination of keys, you can use to issue a command without using the menus.

Ellipsis: Three dots (periods) following a menu command, which indicate that a dialog box will follow.

Selection letter: The underlined letter of the command or menu name. Keyboard users can select a command by typing the selection letter or can select a menu by holding down **Alt** and typing the selection letter.

Basic Word Tasks

USING WORD MENUS

Exercise

Follow these steps to practice choosing menu commands.

1 Click on **F**ormat or press **Alt+O**.

2 Click on Change Cas**e** or press **E**.

```
Format
  Font...
  Paragraph...
  Tabs...
  Borders and Shading...
  Columns...
  Change Case...
  Drop Cap...
  Bullets and Numbering...
  Heading Numbering...
  AutoFormat...
  Style Gallery...
  Style...
  Frame...
  Picture...
  Drawing Object...
```

3 Click on **Cancel** or press **Esc**.

4 Click on **Help** or press **Alt+H**.

5 Click on **A**bout Microsoft Word or press **A**.

6 Click on **OK**, or press **Esc**.

```
Help
  Contents
  Search for Help on...
  Index
  Quick Preview
  Examples and Demos
  Tip of the Day...
  WordPerfect Help...
  Technical Support
  About Microsoft Word...
```

TIP

Oops! If you start to enter a menu command but then change your mind, press **Esc**.

TIP

Another Way Another way to select from the menu once it's open is to press the up or down arrow key on the keyboard until the item you want is highlighted. Then press **Enter** to choose it.

WORKING WITH DIALOG BOXES

What Is a Dialog Box?

A *dialog box* is a window that Word displays on-screen when it needs some information from you. A dialog box is often displayed when you enter a menu command or select certain command buttons. While every dialog box is different, they all share many common components. If you learn how to use these components, you'll be able to use any dialog box you encounter.

You can use your mouse to click on the different parts of the dialog box, or you can use the keyboard by pressing the **Tab** key or pressing **Alt** and choosing selection letters. Once all the settings in the dialog box are the way you want them, you can exit the box to carry out the command or task.

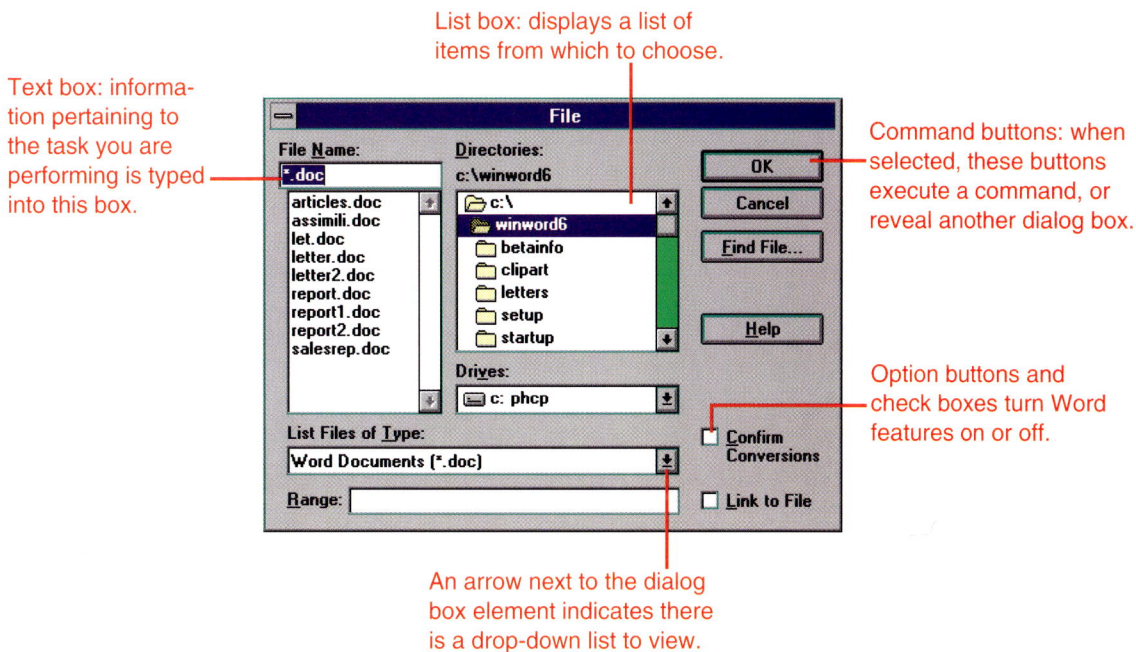

List box: displays a list of items from which to choose.

Text box: information pertaining to the task you are performing is typed into this box.

Command buttons: when selected, these buttons execute a command, or reveal another dialog box.

Option buttons and check boxes turn Word features on or off.

An arrow next to the dialog box element indicates there is a drop-down list to view.

File

File Name:
*.doc

articles.doc
assimili.doc
let.doc
letter.doc
letter2.doc
report.doc
report1.doc
report2.doc
salesrep.doc

Directories:
c:\winword6

c:\
winword6
betainfo
clipart
letters
setup
startup

OK
Cancel
Find File...
Help

Drives:
c: phcp

List Files of Type:
Word Documents (*.doc)

Range:

Confirm Conversions
Link to File

TIP

Dialog Box Mistakes? To return to the document window without making any changes, use the **Cancel** button in the dialog box, or press **Esc**.

Basic Word Tasks

How to Use a Dialog Box

To select any item in a dialog box, click on it or press **Alt** plus the item's selection letter. Once the item is selected, use the item as noted in this table:

Text box. Click or use the left and right arrow keys to position the cursor. Type an entry. Use Del and Backspace to erase, if necessary.

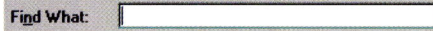

Find What: [   ]

List box. Double-click on the item you want, or use the arrow keys to highlight the item. If the box has scroll bars, click on the scroll arrows to see portions of the list, or use the keyboard arrow keys to scroll.

Regular
Italic
Bold
Bold Italic

Drop-down list. Click on the down arrow to display the list, or press **Alt** plus the selection letter. You can also use the down arrow or the **Spacebar** on the keyboard. Click on the item you want, or highlight the item with the arrow keys.

Auto

Combo box. Enter and edit text in the box as you would in a text box, or click the desired item in the list. If you're using the keyboard, tab to the list box and use the arrow keys to highlight an item. Once highlighted, the list item will appear in the text box.

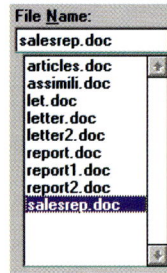

File Name:
salesrep.doc

articles.doc
assimili.doc
let.doc
letter.doc
letter2.doc
report.doc
report1.doc
report2.doc
salesrep.doc

Number box. Enter a number in the box, or click the up and down arrows to increase or decrease the value.

Number of Columns: [1]

Check box. Click on the box to turn it on or off. If you're using the keyboard, press **Alt+**the selection letter.

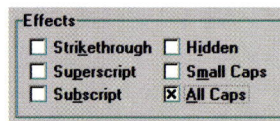

Effects
☐ Strikethrough ☐ Hidden
☐ Superscript ☐ Small Caps
☐ Subscript ☒ All Caps

Option button. Click on a button to turn it on and turn all others in the group off. You can also use the arrow keys on the keyboard.

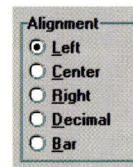

Alignment
⦿ Left
◯ Center
◯ Right
◯ Decimal
◯ Bar

Command button. Click the button to execute or cancel the dialog box selections. Keyboard users can press **Alt** and the selection letters, or tab to the button and press **Enter**.

OK
Cancel

WORKING WITH THE STANDARD TOOLBAR

What Is the Standard Toolbar?

The *Standard toolbar* is a bar across the top of your screen, just below the menu bar, that contains a number of icon buttons, or small graphical images. These buttons represent frequently used Word commands or tasks. The buttons are shortcuts to commands found on the menu lists. Selecting a button from the Standard toolbar can be a lot faster than pulling down menu lists and choosing commands.

To select the Standard toolbar buttons, use the mouse pointer to point and click on the desired button. (Sorry, you can't use the keyboard to select items from the toolbars.) Some buttons will execute a command right away, such as **Paste**. Other buttons, such as the **Save** button, will open a dialog box.

To find out what kind of command or task the button represents, point to the button (but don't click), and look at the status bar. A brief description of the command or task appears. You'll learn more about using the Standard toolbar in Part 2, but it's a good idea to familiarize yourself with what it looks like now so you'll be able to use it later.

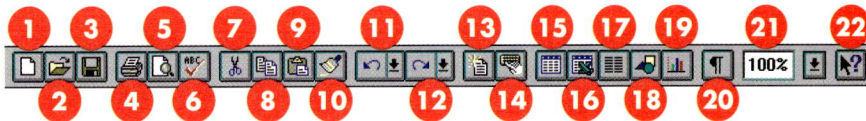

1. Starts a new document.
2. Opens an existing document.
3. Saves the current document.
4. Prints the entire document.
5. Previews the full page.
6. Checks spelling.
7. Cuts selected text to the Clipboard.
8. Copies selected text to the Clipboard.
9. Pastes text from the Clipboard.
10. Copies formatting.
11. Reverses the last action.
12. Reverses the last reversal.
13. Automatically formats a document.
14. Creates or inserts AutoText.
15. Inserts a table.
16. Inserts an Excel worksheet.
17. Changes column format.
18. Opens the Drawing toolbar.
19. Inserts a graph.
20. Shows or hides paragraph marks.
21. Zooms the page view in or out.
22. Activates a Help pointer.

LEARNING THE LINGO

Clipboard: A temporary storage area for text and graphics.

TIP

Unidentified Commands   Some of the toolbar icons represent commands or tasks that are not covered in this book. Please refer to the Word Help system or documentation for more information.

Basic Word Tasks

WORKING WITH THE FORMATTING TOOLBAR

What Is the Formatting Toolbar?

The Formatting toolbar is displayed on your screen between the menu bar and the document, just below the Standard toolbar. Like the Standard toolbar, the Formatting toolbar has icon buttons, or small graphical images. However, the Formatting toolbar buttons quickly initiate certain kinds of formatting commands to apply to your document, and access drop-down menu lists for selecting styles, fonts, and point sizes. You'll find the Formatting toolbar to be a real timesaving tool when you are creating documents.

To choose formatting commands from the Formatting toolbar, just click the appropriate button, or click the arrows on the toolbar to reveal drop-down menu lists. You'll learn more about using the Formatting toolbar features in Part 3.

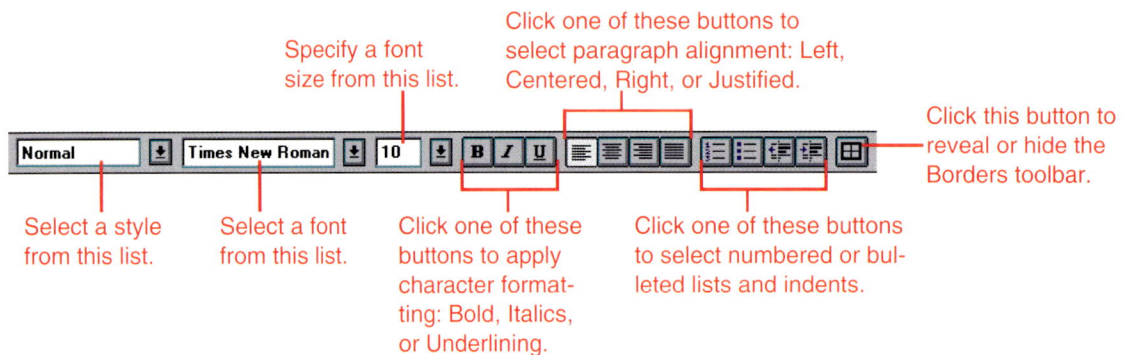

Click one of these buttons to select paragraph alignment: Left, Centered, Right, or Justified.

Specify a font size from this list.

Click this button to reveal or hide the Borders toolbar.

| Normal | Times New Roman | 10 | B I U | | |

Select a style from this list.

Select a font from this list.

Click one of these buttons to apply character formatting: Bold, Italics, or Underlining.

Click one of these buttons to select numbered or bulleted lists and indents.

LEARNING THE LINGO

Formatting: Changing the look of text or positioning of text in a document.

Font: A set of characters that share a particular design style.

Point size: Text characters are measured in points; there are 72 points in an inch.

Alignment: The positioning of text within a document in regard to the left and right margins. Also called *justification*.

TIP

Where's My Formatting Toolbar? If the Formatting toolbar is not visible, issue the **View Toolbars** command and select **Formatting** to display it.

1. Click on **View** or press **Alt+V**.

2. Click on **Toolbars** or press **T**.

3. Select **Formatting**, and click **OK** or press **Enter**.

GETTING HELP FROM WORD

What Is Help?

Help is exactly what it sounds like—on-screen assistance from the Word for Windows program for any problems you encounter. For example, if you were in the midst of saving a document and an unfamiliar dialog box appeared on your screen, you could access the on-line Help feature to find out what to do. Word has a sophisticated Help system that can display information on-screen about any Word task.

There are several Help options to choose from the **H**elp menu, including a glossary and specific information about using Help. The Help system is also *context-sensitive*, meaning that you can get help when you're in the middle of a task. Help knows what point in the program you are seeking help for. It will take you directly to the Help section that explains all about the task you are trying to perform.

Word's Help facility has several unique features that assist you in finding the information you need.

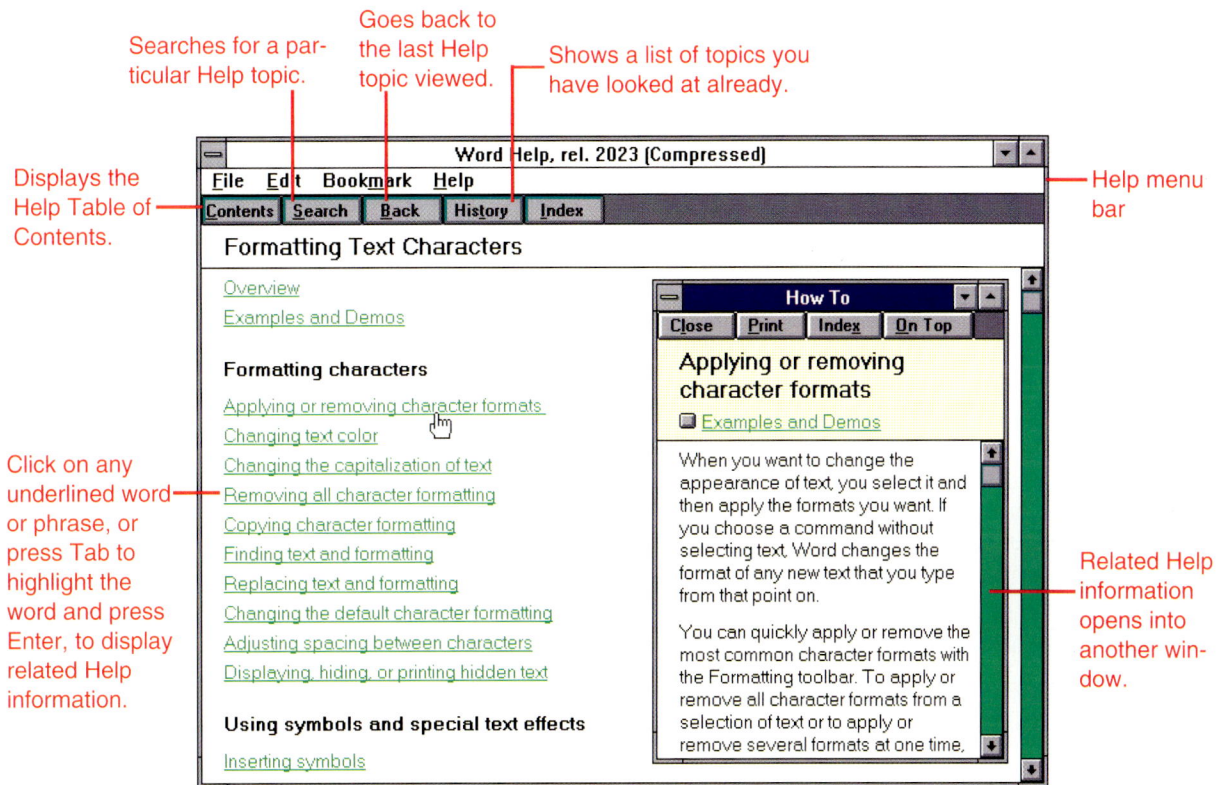

Searches for a particular Help topic.

Goes back to the last Help topic viewed.

Shows a list of topics you have looked at already.

Displays the Help Table of Contents.

Help menu bar

Click on any underlined word or phrase, or press Tab to highlight the word and press Enter, to display related Help information.

Related Help information opens into another window.

Word Help, rel. 2023 (Compressed)

File   Edit   Bookmark   Help

Contents | Search | Back | History | Index

Formatting Text Characters

Overview

Examples and Demos

Formatting characters

Applying or removing character formats

Changing text color

Changing the capitalization of text

Removing all character formatting

Copying character formatting

Finding text and formatting

Replacing text and formatting

Changing the default character formatting

Adjusting spacing between characters

Displaying, hiding, or printing hidden text

Using symbols and special text effects

Inserting symbols

How To

Close | Print | Index | On Top

Applying or removing character formats

Examples and Demos

When you want to change the appearance of text, you select it and then apply the formats you want. If you choose a command without selecting text, Word changes the format of any new text that you type from that point on.

You can quickly apply or remove the most common character formats with the Formatting toolbar. To apply or remove all character formats from a selection of text or to apply or remove several formats at one time,

GETTING HELP FROM WORD

Using Help

1 Press **Alt+H** or click on **Help**.

2 Click on **Contents** or press **C**.

```
Help                          1
Contents                              2
Search for Help on...
Index

Quick Preview
Examples and Demos
Tip of the Day...

WordPerfect Help...
Technical Support

About Microsoft Word...
```

3 Click on an underlined topic to view related information.

4 Click on the **Contents** button or press **C** at any time to return to the Help Contents screen.

```
Word Help, rel. 2023 (Compressed)
File   Edit   Bookmark   Help
4  Contents | Search | Back | History | Index

Word Help Contents
To learn how to use Help, press F1.

Using Word
Step-by-step instructions to help you complete
your tasks

Examples and Demos
Visual examples and demonstrations to help
you learn Word

Reference Information                3
Answers to common questions; tips; and guides
to terminology, commands, and the keyboard

Programming with Microsoft Word
Complete reference information about the
WordBasic macro language

Technical Support
```

5 Click on **File** and **Exit**, or press **Alt+F4** to close Help.

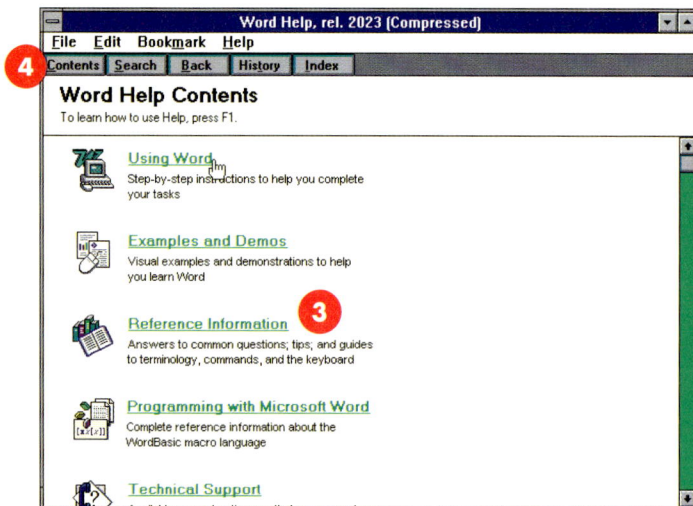

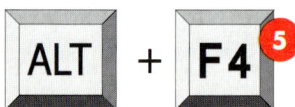

ALT + **F4** **5**

LEARNING THE LINGO

Context-Sensitive: A Help system that takes you directly to the information pertaining to the task you are trying to perform, without routing you through a topical index.

TIP

Toolbar Shortcut   You can also click on the **Help** button on the Standard toolbar to access the Help system. When selected, this option turns your mouse pointer into a question mark icon. Use it to click onto areas of your screen or menus that you would like to know more about.

Exercise

Follow these steps to practice using the Help feature.

1 Click on **Help** or press **Alt+H**.

2 Click on **Contents** or press **C**.

3 Click on the underlined words **Using Word**, or press **Tab** until the word is highlighted and press **Enter**.

4 Click on the underlined words **Typing and Revising**, or press **Tab** until the words are highlighted and press **Enter**.

5 Click on **Inserting text into a document**, or press **Tab** until the phrase is highlighted and press **Enter**.

6 Scroll through the How To window to read about the selected topic. Click on the scroll bar arrows to display different sections of the topic, or use the arrow keys, PgUp, and PgDn keys to view the section with the keyboard.

7 To exit the topic window, click on **Close** or press **Alt+L**.

8 To exit Help, click on **File Exit** or press **Alt+F4**.

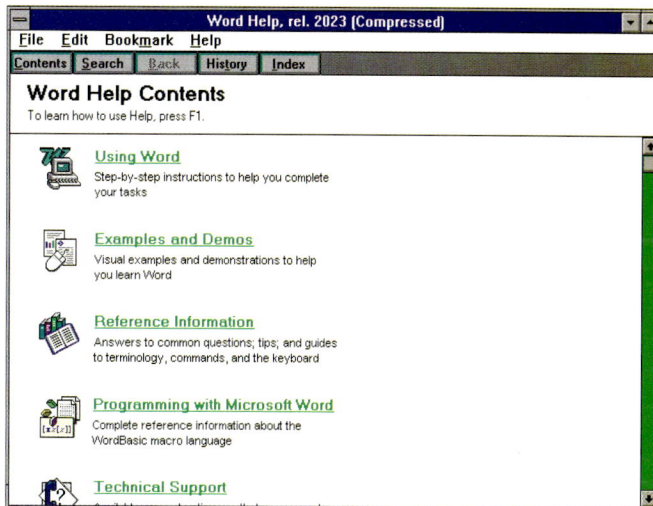

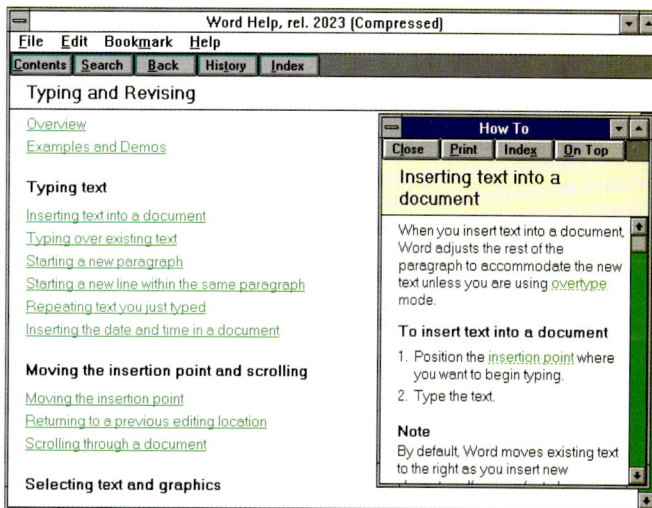

TIP

Fast Help Press **F1** while any dialog box is displayed to see Help information about that dialog box.

TIP

Help Tip At any time while you are viewing Help information, you can select the **C**ontents button to return to the Help Contents screen.

Basic Word Tasks

When Do You Exit Word?

When you're finished working in Word, you should exit the program. This frees up the system resources that Word is using so that you can run a different program. (See the task "Closing a Document" for further information on exiting Word.)

Exiting Word

1 Click on **File** or press **Alt+F**.

2 Click on **Exit** or press **X**.

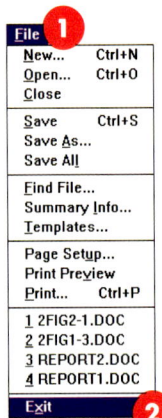

TIP

Exiting Tip   You should always exit Word before you turn off your computer. This ensures that all the Word documents you have created are saved onto disk, so that you can retrieve them later.

TIP

Fast Getaway   If you're using the mouse, you can exit the program quickly by pointing at the program's Control-menu box and double-clicking. If you're using the keyboard, press **Alt+F4**.

TIP

Save Changes to Document?   If you're trying to exit the program without saving your current document, a dialog box will appear, asking you whether you want to save your changes. Click on (or tab to) the **Cancel** button, and you'll return to the document window. Click on **No** or press **N**, and you'll exit without saving. Click on **Yes** or press **Y**, and the Save As dialog box will appear for you to name and save your file. (See the "Saving a Document" task in Part 2.)

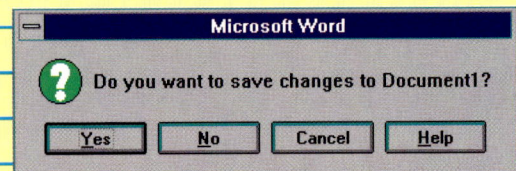

PART 2

Creating, Editing, Saving, and Printing Documents

In this section, you'll learn the basics of creating and editing your Word documents. You'll develop the basic skills needed to work with any Word document, including how to save, print, and close documents.

You'll learn about:

- Entering Text
- Moving Around the Document Window
- Using Insert and Overstrike Modes
- Correcting Mistakes
- Selecting Text
- Deleting Text
- Moving and Copying Text
- Saving a Document

- Opening a Document
- Closing a Document
- Finding and Replacing Text
- Zooming In and Out
- Working with Multiple Documents
- Printing a Document
- Using Print Preview

ENTERING TEXT

How Do You Enter Text?

When you start Word for Windows, your screen displays a new document, ready and waiting to go. Entering text is quite simple—just start typing. The open area on your screen is where your text appears, and the blinking line that shows where characters will appear on-screen is called the *cursor*, or *insertion point*.

You can move the insertion point by moving the mouse pointer to a new position and clicking the cursor into place, or by using the arrow keys on the keyboard. As you type, the cursor moves to the right, advancing automatically to the next line when you've run out of room. This means you don't have to press the Enter key to signify a new line. Word "wraps" your sentence to the next line automatically. The only time you need to press the Enter key is when you're ready to begin a new paragraph.

Word documents are broken down into paragraphs. A paragraph can be a single line, a grouping of text, or even bulleted copy.

The cursor, or insertion point

A regular text block paragraph

A heading is also a paragraph.

Each bulleted list item is a paragraph too.

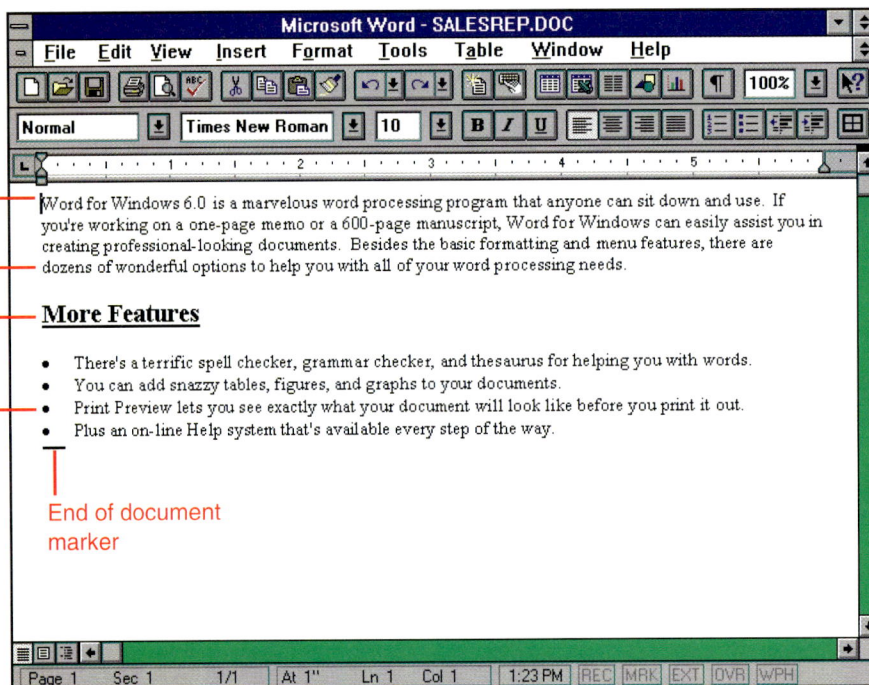

End of document marker

TIP

Hard and Soft Returns When you press Enter at the end of a line, it's considered a *hard return*.

This allows you to begin a new line of text in a new paragraph. When you let Word wrap text at the end of the line, it's called a *soft return*.

Typing Text

1 Type your text.

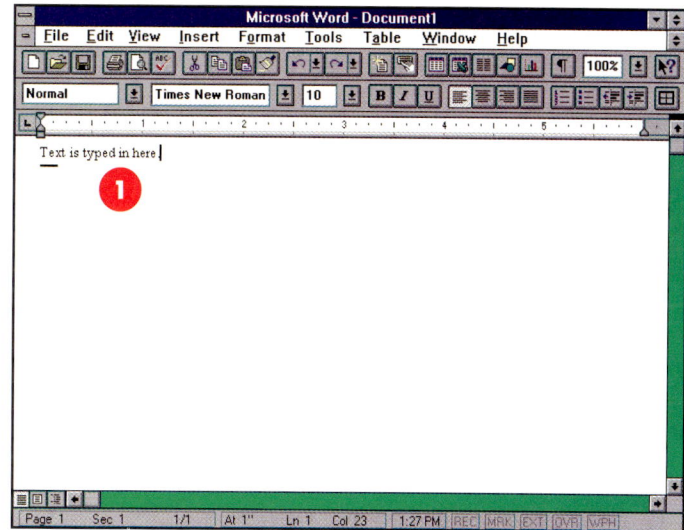

2 Press **Enter** at the end of a paragraph.

ENTER **2**

TIP

Text Tips   To insert a blank line into your document, just press **Enter** as many times as needed.

ENTER

To indent a line of text, press **Tab**.

TAB

LEARNING THE LINGO

Document: The text that you are writing or editing—a letter, memo, report, and so on. No matter how many or how few characters, each group of text saved together in a file is a document.

Cursor: A blinking vertical line that indicates where typed characters will appear; also known as the *insertion point*.

Wrapping: When your text reaches the end of a line, the cursor moves to the start of the next line automatically.

Paragraph: A group of words that is treated as a block of text. Paragraphs can also be single lines, captions, bulleted text, and even blank lines. A paragraph is created by pressing the Enter key at the end of a line.

Bulleted list: A text list with bullet symbols, or small dots, in front of each line. Bulleted lists are used to emphasize text in your document.

End of document marker: A short horizontal line that marks the end of the document.

29

Creating, Editing, Saving, and Printing Documents

ENTERING TEXT

Exercise

To practice entering text and moving the cursor across the screen, enter the text shown here, and then follow the steps below.

1 Type the date and press **Enter** four times.

2 Type **Dear Mr. Williams:** and press **Enter** twice.

3 Type the two sentences of the letter, and then press **Enter** four times.

4 Type **Sincerely,** and press **Enter** four times.

5 Type your name.

6 Position the cursor immediately after the word "Friday" in the first sentence, and then type a comma.

7 Position the cursor immediately after the last sentence, and then type **We look forward to your attendance.**

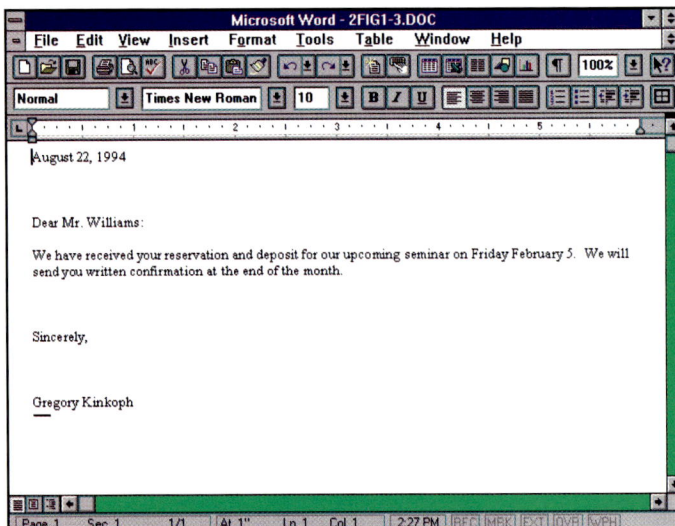

Microsoft Word - 2FIG1-3.DOC

File Edit View Insert Format Tools Table Window Help

Normal   Times New Roman   10   B I U

August 22, 1994

Dear Mr. Williams:

We have received your reservation and deposit for our upcoming seminar on Friday February 5. We will send you written confirmation at the end of the month.

Sincerely,

Gregory Kinkoph

Page 1   Sec 1   1/1   At 1"   Ln 1   Col 1   2:27 PM   REC MRK EXT OVR WPH

TIP

Opening a New Document   To open a new document in which to type, use the **N**ew command.

Click on **File** or press **Alt+F**. Click on **N**ew or press **N**. Then click **OK** or press **Enter**. A new document

will appear in your window. You can also click on the **New**

Document button located on the Standard toolbar.

TIP

Need a New Page?   To insert a page break in your document, follow these steps:

1. Move the cursor to where you want the page break to occur.
2. Click on **I**nsert or press **Alt+I**.
3. Click on **B**reak or press **B**.
4. A dialog box will appear for you to choose what kind of break to insert. Make your selection and click **OK**, or press **Enter**.

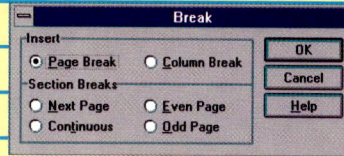

```
┌──────────────── Break ────────────────┐
│ ┌─Insert──────────────────────┐  ┌────────┐
│ │ ⦿ Page Break  ○ Column Break │  │   OK   │
│ │ ─Section Breaks──────────────│  ├────────┤
│ │ ○ Next Page   ○ Even Page    │  │ Cancel │
│ │ ○ Continuous  ○ Odd Page     │  ├────────┤
│ └──────────────────────────────┘  │  Help  │
│                                    └────────┘
└────────────────────────────────────────────┘
```

A ruled line will appear in your document, indicating where the page break occurs.

TIP

Template Tips   Word for Windows comes with numerous predefined templates you can readily use, ranging from a memo to a purchase order. *Templates* are simply files that have formatting and styles already in place. All you have to do is add the text. To learn more about using templates, see the tasks "Working with Templates" and "Creating a Template" in Part 4.

Creating, Editing, Saving, and Printing Documents

MOVING AROUND THE DOCUMENT WINDOW

Why Move Around the Document?

Once you have entered text into your document, you'll invariably have occasions to make changes. To change (or *edit*) your text, you'll need to know how to move around in the document window.

When moving the mouse pointer around the document window, you'll notice it changes appearance, depending on where it's located on the screen. When the mouse pointer is located in the text area of your document, it will look like a capital "I." This is called an *I-beam*. When the mouse pointer is moved anywhere outside the text area, it becomes a small arrow. At the left side of the text area is an invisible *selection bar*, just to the left of the margin. The mouse pointer becomes an arrow pointing northeast when placed here as well.

When inside the text area, you can place the cursor by moving the mouse pointer to a new position and clicking the cursor into place. To make selections outside the text area, move the mouse pointer and click on the elements you want to select.

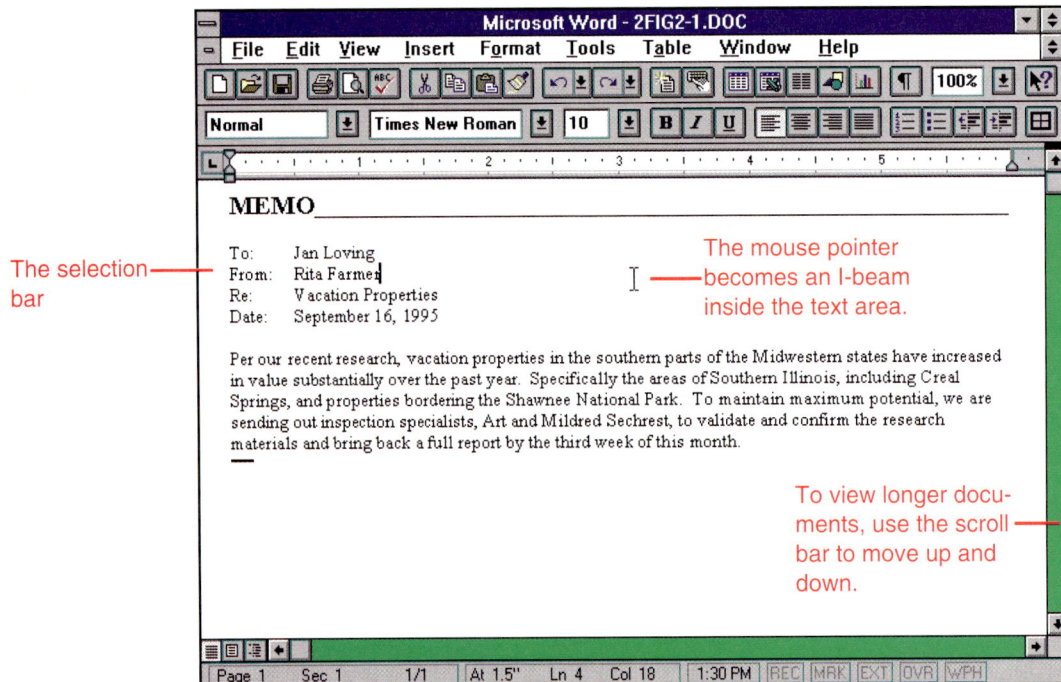

The selection bar

The mouse pointer becomes an I-beam inside the text area.

To view longer documents, use the scroll bar to move up and down.

Moving Around with the Keyboard

You can move around the document window with the keyboard by pressing the *cursor movement keys* (such as the arrow keys) or *combination keys* (such as **Ctrl+Home**).

You can move the insertion point by clicking in the new location. You can also move the insertion point using the keyboard.

Press...	To move...
← or →	Left or right one character
CTRL + ← or CTRL + →	Left or right one word
HOME	To the beginning of the line
END	To the end of the line
↑ or ↓	Up or down one line
CTRL + ↑ or CTRL + ↓	Up or down one paragraph
PG UP or PG DN	Up or down one screen
CTRL + HOME	To the start of the document
CTRL + END	To the end of the document
CTRL + PG UP	To the top of the screen
CTRL + PG DN	To the bottom of the screen

MOVING AROUND THE DOCUMENT WINDOW

LEARNING THE LINGO

Edit: To make changes in your text, or otherwise modify your document.

I-beam: The capital-I shape that the mouse pointer takes on when it is anywhere inside the text area of your screen.

Selection bar: The narrow area to the left of the left margin, used to select blocks of text. When you place the mouse pointer here, it turns into an arrow.

QUICK REFRESHER

Here are the mouse techniques you will need to use to move around the document window:

Point: To move your mouse so that the arrow on-screen is directly over the item you want to select.

Click: To press the left mouse button while holding the mouse pointer steadily over the item to be selected.

Double-click: To quickly press the left mouse button twice in rapid succession.

Drag: To press and hold the mouse button, and then move the mouse to a new position before releasing the button.

INSERT AND OVERSTRIKE MODES

When to Use Insert and Overstrike Mode

Word has two methods for entering text. In *Insert* mode, existing text moves over to the right to make room for the new text you're typing. In *Overstrike* (or *Type-over*) mode, existing text is replaced (written over) by new text on a character-by-character basis (this is applicable only when there is text to the right of the insertion point). When the Overstrike mode is on, you'll see the letters **OVR** (for Overstrike) in bold on the status bar.

Entering Text in Insert and Overstrike Modes

1 Move the cursor to where you want new text to appear.

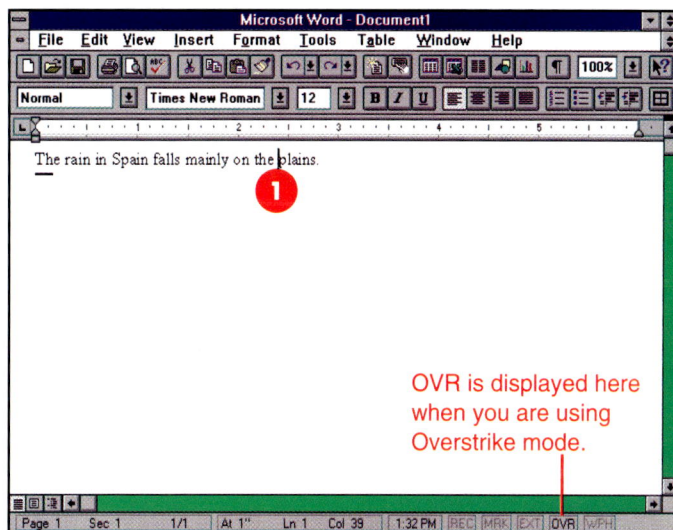

OVR is displayed here when you are using Overstrike mode.

2 Press the **Insert** key to switch back and forth between Insert and Overstrike modes.

TIP

Insert by Default When you start Word for Windows 6.0, it's always in Insert mode unless you change it to Overstrike mode.

LEARNING THE LINGO

Insert mode: Adding text between existing text without deleting any existing characters. Existing text is shifted to the right as new text is typed.

Overstrike mode: Adding text that takes the place of (types over) existing text; also called *Typeover* mode.

INSERT AND OVERSTRIKE MODES

Exercise

To practice using the Insert and Overstrike modes, enter the text shown in the figure and follow these steps.

1 Change to Overstrike mode by pressing **Insert**, move the cursor to the left of the number 4 at the end of the date, and then type a **3**.

2 Press **Insert** to change the mode back to Insert mode, and move the cursor to the beginning of the word "contribution" in the first sentence. Type **generous** and press the Spacebar.

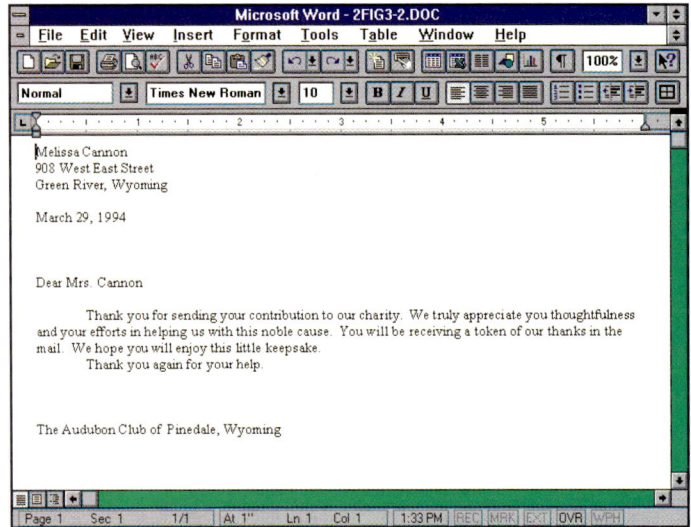

CORRECTING MISTAKES

How Do You Correct Text?

A timesaving feature of any word processing program is the ability to correct mistakes. With Word for Windows, you can fix errors easily using the mouse or keyboard. To fix minor mistakes, use the Delete and Backspace keys.

Correcting Text

1 Move the cursor to the text you want to delete.

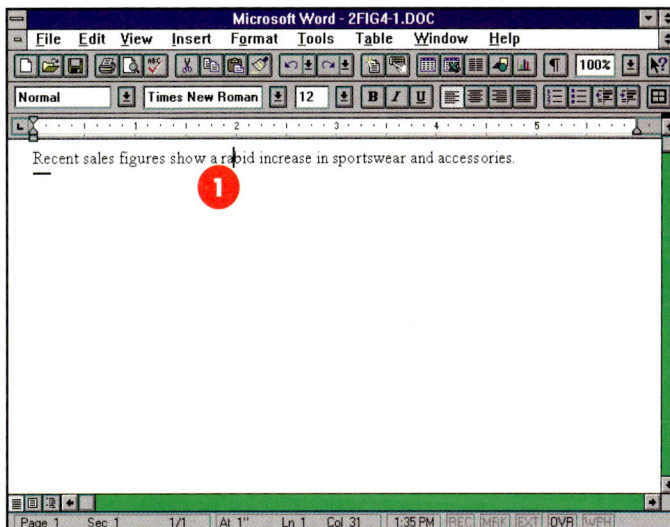

2 Press **Delete** to erase a character to the right of the cursor, or press **Backspace** to erase a character to the left of the cursor.

> **TIP**
>
> **Erasing Trick** If you hold down the **Delete** or **Backspace** keys, you can quickly delete more than one character at a time. But be careful—it goes really fast, and you might erase more characters than you intended!

CORRECTING MISTAKES

Exercise

Type in the sentence shown in the figure, and follow these steps to practice using the Delete and Backspace keys.

1 Position the cursor to the right of the comma.

2 Press **Backspace** until the words "to be," are deleted.

3 Position the cursor at the beginning of the word "the."

4 Press **Delete** until the words "the question" are erased.

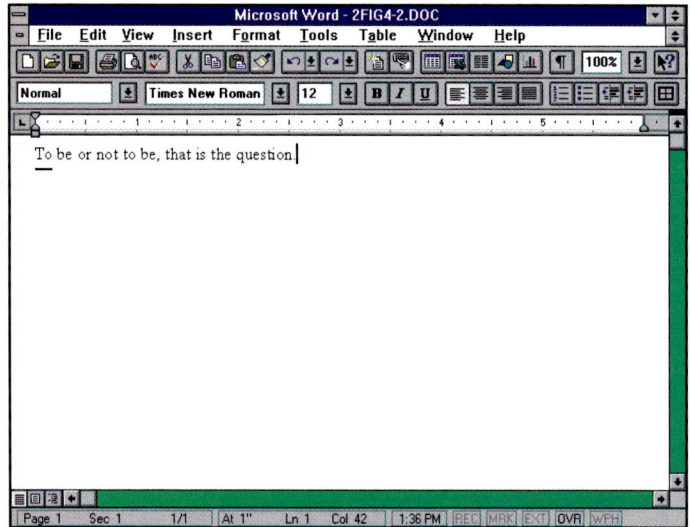

SELECTING TEXT

Why Select Text?

To edit (that is, change) larger portions of your text, you must learn to select the text portion you wish to modify. Anytime you want to move or copy text or assign formatting to a paragraph, you must first *select* (or *highlight*) the text portion you want to change.

Selected text has a solid block of black surrounding the word or words. Instead of black characters on a white background, highlighted text shows white characters on a black background. (It's also called *reversed text*.)

You can select a character, a word, a sentence, a paragraph, or an entire document. The selected text is called a *text block*. Once a text block has been selected, various command functions can be applied to the highlighted text.

Selected text is highlighted in black. —

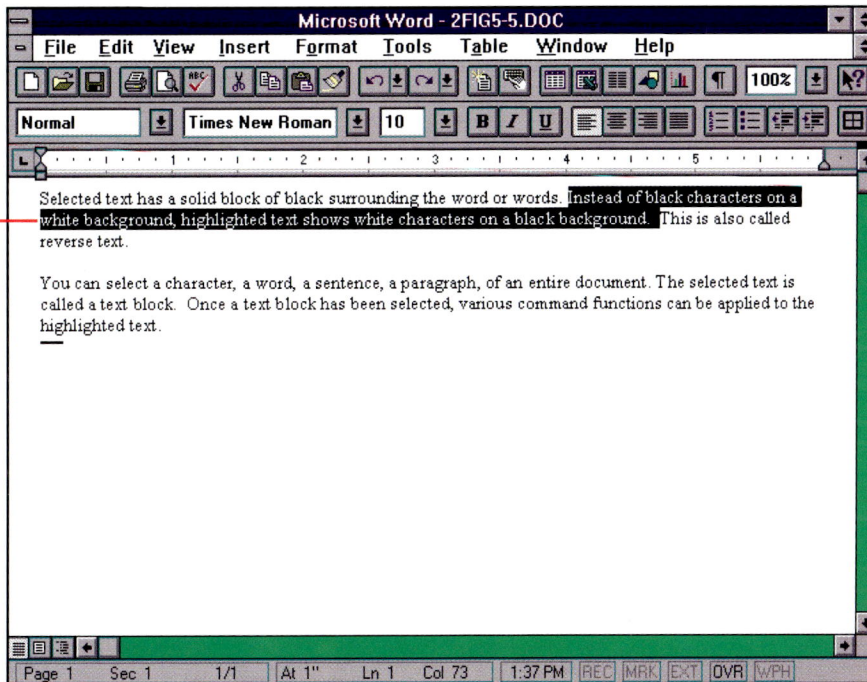

Microsoft Word - 2FIG5-5.DOC

File Edit View Insert Format Tools Table Window Help

`Normal` `Times New Roman` `10` `B` `I` `U`

Selected text has a solid block of black surrounding the word or words. Instead of black characters on a white background, highlighted text shows white characters on a black background. This is also called reverse text.

You can select a character, a word, a sentence, a paragraph, of an entire document. The selected text is called a text block. Once a text block has been selected, various command functions can be applied to the highlighted text.

`Page 1   Sec 1   1/1   At 1"   Ln 1   Col 73   1:37 PM   REC MRK EXT OVR WPH`

LEARNING THE LINGO

Highlight: A black background or bar that surrounds a word or group of words indicating that the text is selected and commands can be executed that will affect that text.

Text block: Any amount of text, ranging from a single character to an entire document, that you want to work with.

Formatting: Changing the look of text, such as making it bolder, larger, or changing its positioning.

Creating, Editing, Saving, and Printing Documents

39

SELECTING TEXT

Selecting Text with the Mouse

1 Point to the first letter of the text block you want to select.

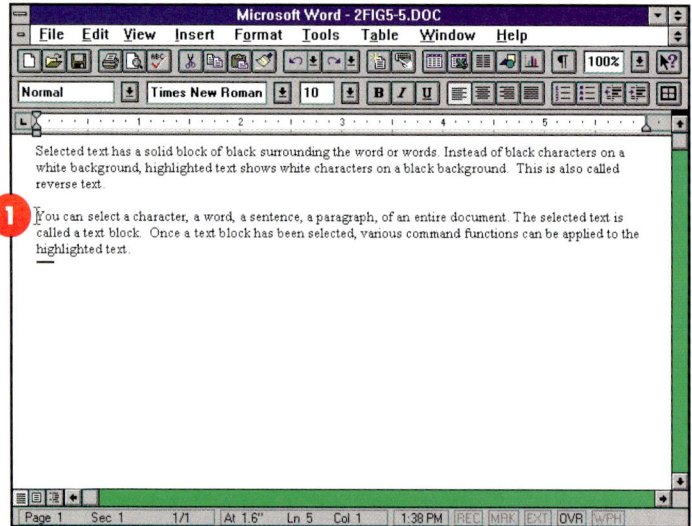

2 Press and hold down the left mouse button, drag the mouse pointer to the last character of text you want highlighted, and then release the mouse button.

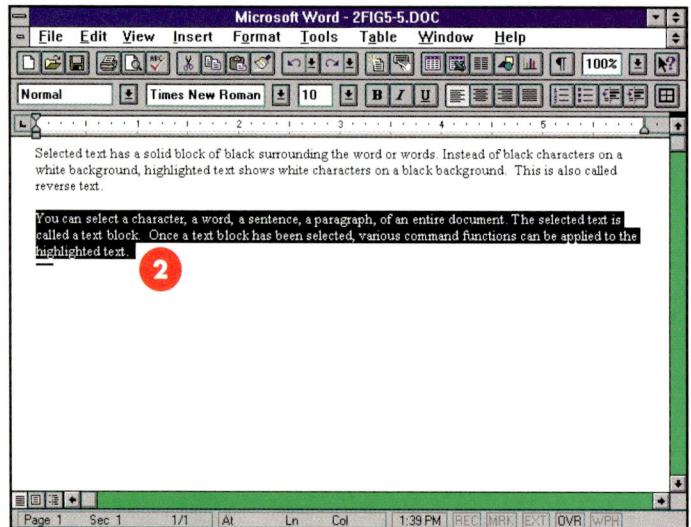

TIP

The Invisible Selection Bar

You can use an invisible selection bar at the left side of your left margin to select blocks of text. When moved to this area, the mouse pointer becomes an arrow that points northeast. Use clicking or dragging motions to quickly highlight blocks of text.

TIP

Quick Select   To select a word quickly, move the mouse pointer to the word and double-click. To select a sentence, press and hold Ctrl and click anywhere in the sentence.

40

Selecting Text with the Keyboard

1 With the arrow keys, move the insertion point to the beginning of the text block you want to select.

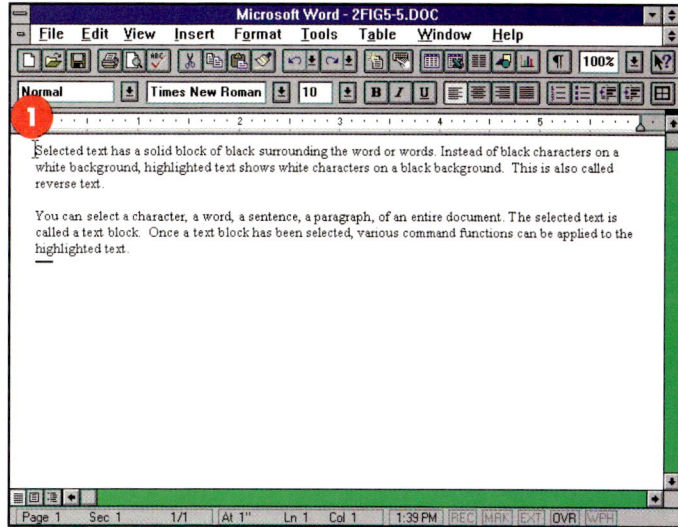

Selected text has a solid block of black surrounding the word or words. Instead of black characters on a white background, highlighted text shows white characters on a black background. This is also called reverse text.

You can select a character, a word, a sentence, a paragraph, of an entire document. The selected text is called a text block. Once a text block has been selected, various command functions can be applied to the highlighted text.

2 Press and hold the **Shift** key.

SHIFT

3 Press the arrow keys or any of the cursor movement keys and key combinations to highlight the text you want to select. Stop highlighting when the last letter of the text block has been selected; then release the **Shift** key.

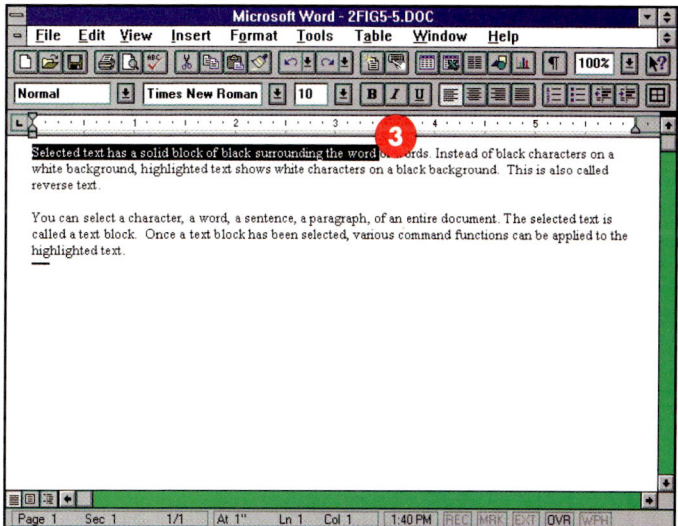

Selected text has a solid block of black surrounding the word or words. Instead of black characters on a white background, highlighted text shows white characters on a black background. This is also called reverse text.

You can select a character, a word, a sentence, a paragraph, of an entire document. The selected text is called a text block. Once a text block has been selected, various command functions can be applied to the highlighted text.

41

SELECTING TEXT

TIP

Select the Wrong Text? If you've accidentally highlighted some text you don't want to select, click anywhere in the document or press an arrow key to cancel the selection.

TIP

The Select All Command You can quickly select your entire document by pulling down the **E**dit menu and using the Select All command.

1. Click on **E**dit or press **Alt+E**.
2. Click on Select All or press **L**.

DELETING TEXT

What's the Best Way to Delete Text?

In the task "Correcting Mistakes," you learned how to delete small amounts of text using the **Delete** and **Backspace** keys. Pecking away at the **Delete** or **Backspace** keys is a slow process when you need to erase larger amounts of text. An easier method is to delete *blocks* of text.

Before you can delete a block of text, you must first select or highlight it. To learn how to select text, turn to the "Selecting Text" task found earlier in this section.

Deleting Text

1 Select the text to be deleted.

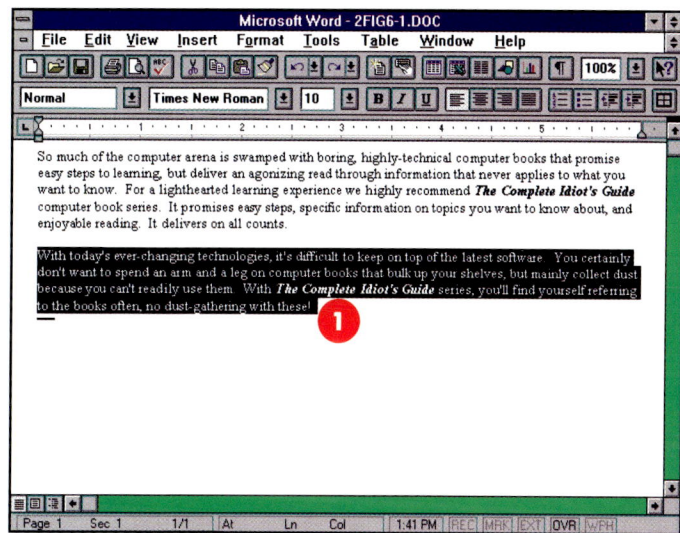

2 Press **Delete**.

TIP

Quick Delete and Replace   If you plan to replace a section of existing text with new text, you can perform an easy *delete and replace* action. Select the text block to be deleted and just start typing. The selected text block disappears and is replaced by what you type.

DELETING TEXT

Exercise

Type in the text shown in the figure, and practice deleting a block of text by following these steps:

1 Position the cursor at the beginning of the second paragraph.

2 Press and drag the mouse until the entire paragraph is selected, and then release the mouse button. If you are using the keyboard, use the arrow keys to highlight the block.

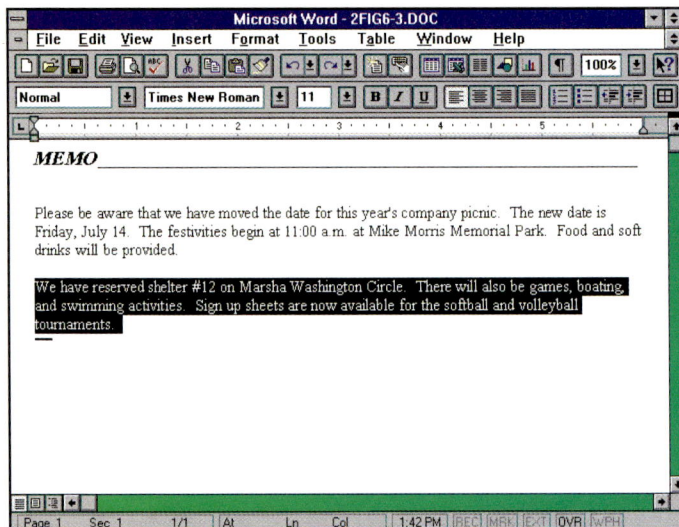

3 Press **Delete**.

Microsoft Word - 2FIG6-3.DOC

File Edit View Insert Format Tools Table Window Help

Normal   Times New Roman   11   B I U   100%

MEMO

Please be aware that we have moved the date for this year's company picnic. The new date is Friday, July 14. The festivities begin at 11:00 a.m. at Mike Morris Memorial Park. Food and soft drinks will be provided.

We have reserved shelter #12 on Marsha Washington Circle. There will also be games, boating, and swimming activities. Sign up sheets are now available for the softball and volleyball tournaments.

Page 1   Sec 1   1/1   At   Ln   Col   1:42 PM   REC   MRK   EXT   OVR   WPH

TIP

Undeleting Text If you've accidentally deleted text you didn't mean to delete, use the Undo command to restore your text.

1. Click on **E**dit or press **Alt+E**.

2. Click on **U**ndo Typing or press **U**.

You can also use the Undo buttons on the Standard toolbar.

Reverses last action   Undoes last Undo action

QUICK REFRESHER

To select text with the mouse

1. Move the pointer to the start of the text.

2. Press and hold the mouse button.

3. Drag the highlight to the end of the text.

4. Release the mouse button.

To select text with the keyboard

1. Move the insertion point to the start of the text.

2. Press and hold **Shift**.

3. Move the insertion point to the end of the text.

4. Release the Shift key.

MOVING AND COPYING TEXT

Why Move or Copy Text?

A marvelous feature of word processing programs is the ability to move and copy text in a document without retyping. For example, you might want to move a paragraph from the middle to the beginning of your document, or from one document into another. Or you might want to duplicate a text block somewhere else in your document.

When text is moved or copied, it's held in a temporary storage area called the *Clipboard*. When you're ready to place the text in another part of your document, it's moved or copied from the Clipboard to your current cursor position. You can use the Clipboard to move and copy text to other documents, or to other Windows programs.

Moving and Copying Text

1 Select the text you want to move or copy.

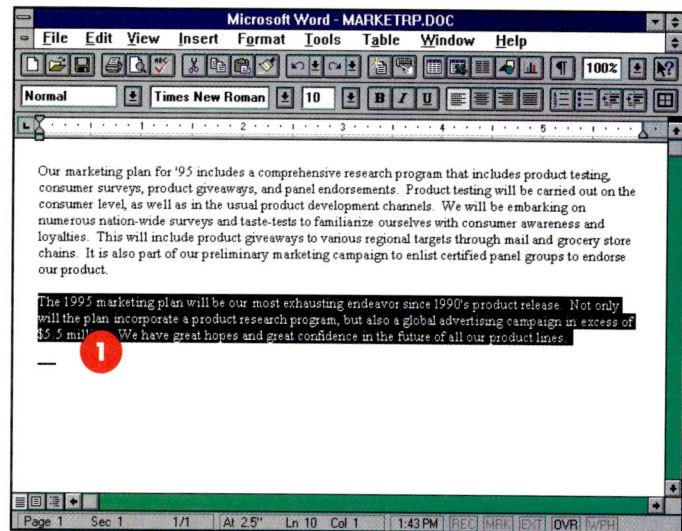

2 Click on **E**dit or press **Alt+E**.

3 Click on C**u**t or press **T** to move text. Click on **C**opy or press **C** to copy text.

MOVING AND COPYING TEXT

4 Move the cursor to where you want the text to appear.

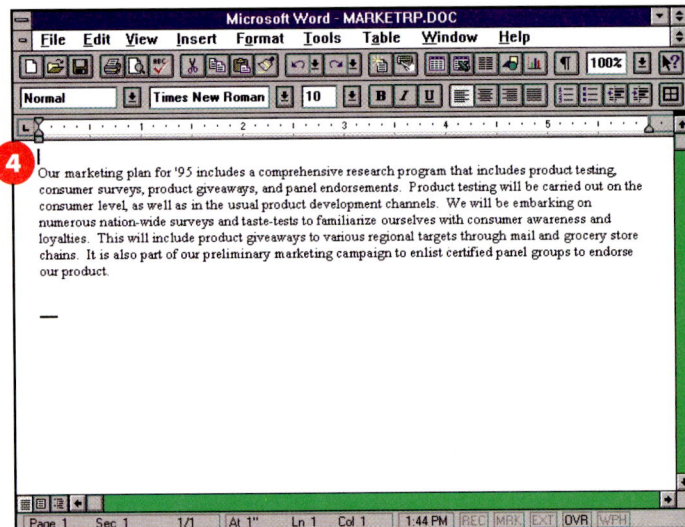

Microsoft Word - MARKETRP.DOC

File Edit View Insert Format Tools Table Window Help

Normal   Times New Roman   10   B I U

4 Our marketing plan for '95 includes a comprehensive research program that includes product testing, consumer surveys, product giveaways, and panel endorsements. Product testing will be carried out on the consumer level, as well as in the usual product development channels. We will be embarking on numerous nation-wide surveys and taste-tests to familiarize ourselves with consumer awareness and loyalties. This will include product giveaways to various regional targets through mail and grocery store chains. It is also part of our preliminary marketing campaign to enlist certified panel groups to endorse our product.

Page 1   Sec 1   1/1   At 1"   Ln 1   Col 1   1:44 PM   REC MRK EXT OVR WPH

5 Click on **E**dit or press **Alt+E**.

6 Click on **P**aste or press **P**.

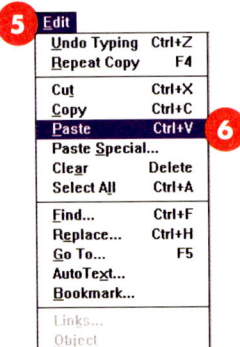

5 Edit

Undo Typing	Ctrl+Z
Repeat Copy	F4
Cut	Ctrl+X
Copy	Ctrl+C
Paste	Ctrl+V	**6**
Paste Special...	
Clear	Delete
Select All	Ctrl+A
Find...	Ctrl+F
Replace...	Ctrl+H
Go To...	F5
AutoText...	
Bookmark...	
Links...	
Object	

TIP

Cut, Copy, and Paste Shortcuts

If you're using the keyboard to enter commands, here are some shortcut keys to cutting, copying, and pasting. Instead of activating the **E**dit menu, press **Ctrl+X** to cut; press **Ctrl+C** to copy; and press **Ctrl+V** to paste.

TIP

Toolbar Shortcuts   You can perform a quick cut, copy, and paste with the Standard toolbar buttons.

To cut, select text and click on the **Cut** button.   Cut button

To copy, select text and click on the **Copy** button.   Copy button

To paste, click the cursor into place, and then click on the **Paste** button.   Paste button

46

Exercise

Enter the text shown, and then practice moving a block of text by following these steps:

1 Move the cursor to the beginning of the second paragraph.

2 Select the entire paragraph. To select with the mouse, press and hold the left mouse button, drag the mouse until the entire paragraph is highlighted, and then release the mouse button. If you are using the keyboard, use the arrow keys to highlight the block.

3 Click on **E**dit or press **Alt+E**.

4 Click on Cu**t** or press **T**.

5 Position the cursor at the beginning of the document.

6 Click on **E**dit or press **Alt+E**.

7 Click on **P**aste or press **P**.

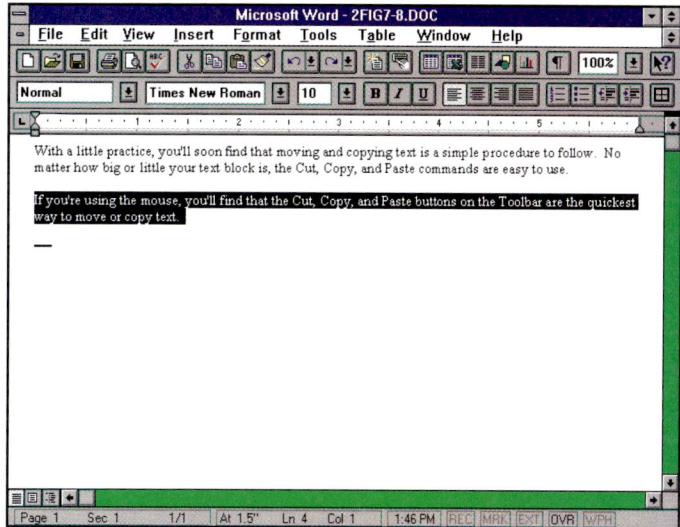

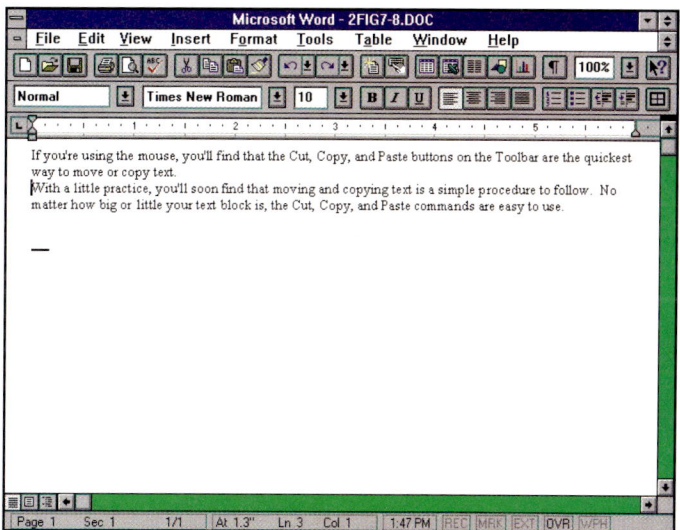

MOVING AND COPYING TEXT

SAVING A DOCUMENT

When Is Saving Necessary?

Whenever you're ready to quit the program and want to keep all your work intact, it's time to save your document. Unless you save your document, everything is "forgotten" by the computer when you turn it off. When you save a document, you can store it on your computer's hard disk or on a floppy disk. When you save your document, or file, you must give it a name.

In Word for Windows, the *file name* can be up to eight characters long. File names can be descriptive, such as MEMO1 or REPORT. You can also add a *file extension* to your document name. SMITH.LTR, for example, has a .LTR extension indicating the document is a letter. File extensions can help you organize your files by type. This is helpful when you are looking for files later. Extensions begin with a period, and are up to three characters long. Unless specified, Word for Windows automatically gives your file names a .DOC extension.

You use the Save **As** command from the **File** menu to save your document for the first time. If you're saving an existing document, you can use the **S**ave command from the **File** menu.

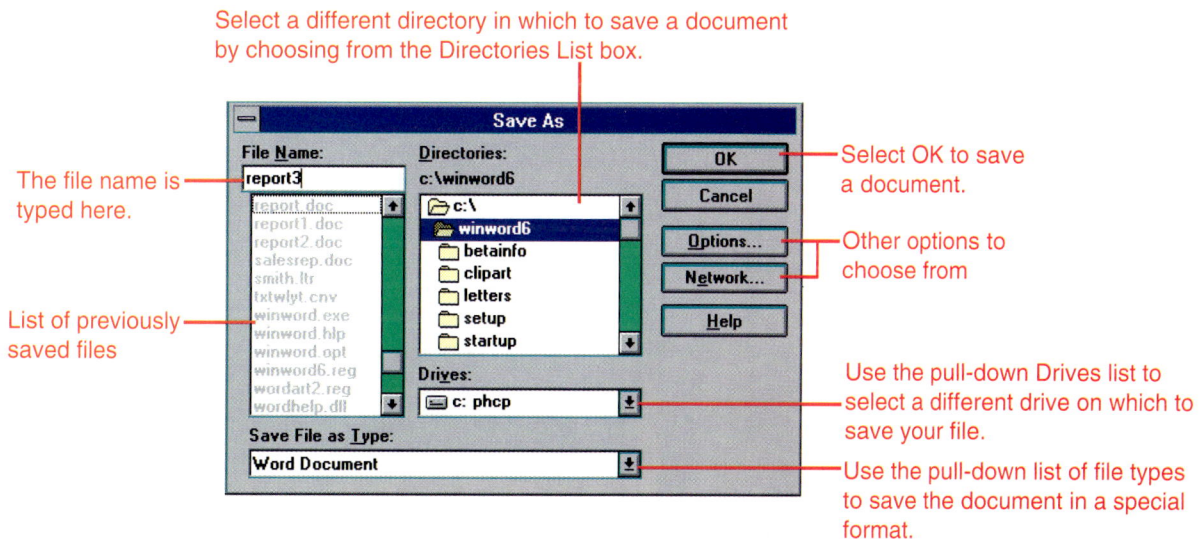

Select a different directory in which to save a document by choosing from the Directories List box.

The file name is typed here.

List of previously saved files

Select OK to save a document.

Other options to choose from

Use the pull-down Drives list to select a different drive on which to save your file.

Use the pull-down list of file types to save the document in a special format.

Save As

File **N**ame: report3

Directories: c:\winword6

report.doc
report1.doc
report2.doc
salesrep.doc
smith.ltr
txtwlyt.cnv
winword.exe
winword.hlp
winword.opt
winword6.reg
wordart2.reg
wordhelp.dll

c:\
winword6
betainfo
clipart
letters
setup
startup

OK
Cancel
Options...
Network...
Help

Dri**v**es: c: phcp

Save File as **T**ype: Word Document

TIP

Saving Tip   It's a good idea to save the document even as you are working on it—and frequently.

If the power goes out and you haven't saved your document, you will lose all your work. It's a terribly frustrating experience!

49

Creating, Editing, Saving, and Printing Documents

SAVING A DOCUMENT

Saving and Naming a Document

1 Click on the **File** menu or press **Alt+F**.

2 Click on Save **As** or press **A**.

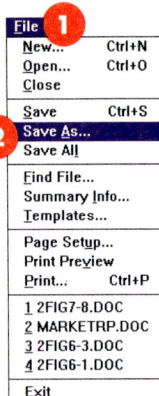

File
New...	Ctrl+N
Open...	Ctrl+O
Close	
Save	Ctrl+S
Save As...	
Save All	
Find File...	
Summary Info...	
Templates...	
Page Setup...	
Print Preview	
Print...	Ctrl+P
1 2FIG7-8.DOC	
2 MARKETRP.DOC	
3 2FIG6-3.DOC	
4 2FIG6-1.DOC	
Exit	

3 Enter a file name for the document.

4 Change the directory, drive, or file type if necessary.

5 Click on **OK** or press **Enter**.

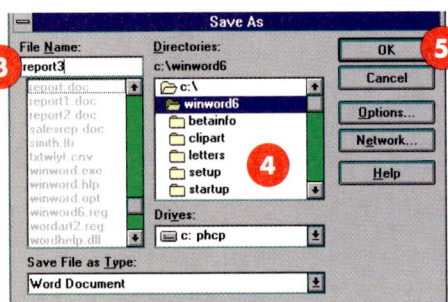

Save As

File Name: report3

report.doc
report1.doc
report2.doc
salesrep.doc
smith.ltr
txtwlyt.cnv
winword.exe
winword.hlp
winword.opt
winword6.reg
wordart2.reg
wordhelp.dll

Directories:
c:\winword6

c:\
winword6
betainfo
clipart
letters
setup
startup

Drives:
c: phcp

Save File as Type:
Word Document

OK
Cancel
Options...
Network...
Help

TIP

Quick Save You can quickly save your document by pressing **Shift+F12** on the keyboard.

LEARNING THE LINGO

File: Whenever you save a document, the information is saved in a file. Files are given unique names that distinguish them from other files.

File extension: An extra name added to a file name that helps determine what kind of file it is, such as .LTR (SMITH.LTR) or .DOC (REPORT.DOC).

TIP

Toolbar Shortcut You can perform a quick save for a new document (or an existing document) by pressing the **Save** button on the Standard toolbar. If the document is new, the Save As dialog box will appear, and you can name your file. If the document has been saved before, Word for Windows saves it automatically and nothing appears on your screen.

50

TIP

What's the Difference Between the Save and the Save As Commands? The Save **A**s command lets you save your document under a new name. The **S**ave command saves the document under its existing name.

Sometimes you may wish to make slight changes to a document (such as a salutation or date) and give the changed document a new name but keep the original intact. The Save **A**s command allows you to do just that. For example, perhaps you have written a letter addressed to Mr. Smith, and you've named that file SMITH.LTR. You want to use that same letter and send it to Ms. Jones. With the Save **A**s command, you can change the address to "Ms. Jones" and save the slightly altered file under a new name, while still retaining the original SMITH.LTR file.

On the other hand, if you're simply updating an existing document, using the **S**ave command will save the updated document under the original file name.

TIP

Saving Under Different Directories Word for Windows saves your document files automatically in the **c:\winword6** directory. If you want to save your document in another directory, select a directory from the **D**irectories list box when the Save As dialog box appears.

Double-click on the root directory to reveal a list of directories.

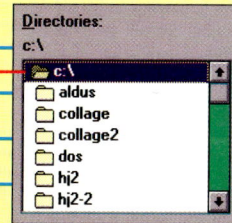

Directories:
c:\
- 🗁 c:\
  - 🗀 aldus
  - 🗀 collage
  - 🗀 collage2
  - 🗀 dos
  - 🗀 hj2
  - 🗀 hj2-2

Creating, Editing, Saving, and Printing Documents

OPENING A DOCUMENT

Why Open a Document?

Unless you plan to create new documents every time you work with Word for Windows, it's a good idea to learn how to open the documents you've saved. The **O**pen command, located in the **F**ile menu, allows you to open files you have previously worked on, as well as files from other directories.

When you select the **O**pen command, a dialog box appears with a list of files to open. Word displays the **c:\winword6** directory automatically when you select the **O**pen command. You can change directories, locate specific file names, display file types, and change drives. Once you've found the file you're looking for, you can open it and begin working on it again.

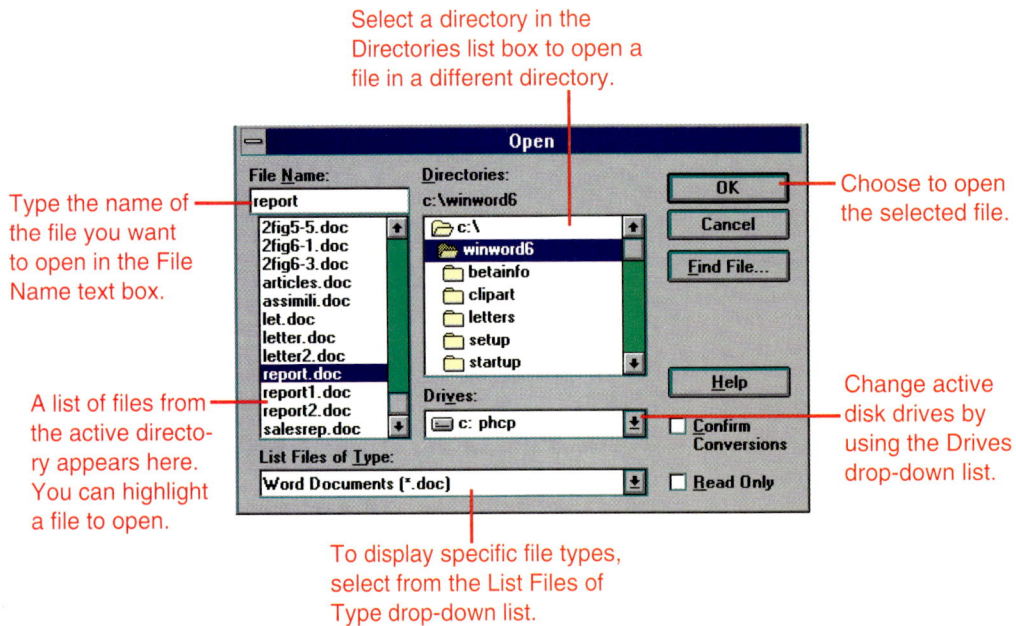

Select a directory in the Directories list box to open a file in a different directory.

Type the name of the file you want to open in the File Name text box.

A list of files from the active directory appears here. You can highlight a file to open.

Choose to open the selected file.

Change active disk drives by using the Drives drop-down list.

To display specific file types, select from the List Files of Type drop-down list.

TIP

Opening Tip When you open another file without closing the document you were working with, the new file appears in your document window. The old file is there, too—you just can't see it.

TIP

Opening Shortcuts You can quickly display the Open dialog box by pressing **Ctrl+F12** or by clicking the **Open** button on the Standard toolbar.

Opening a Document

1 Click on **File** or press **Alt+F**.

2 Click on **Open** or press **O**.

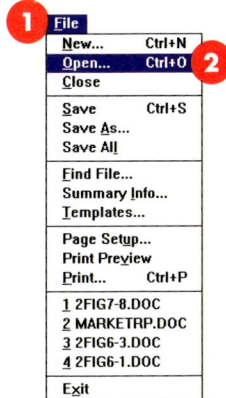

File	
New...	Ctrl+N
Open...	Ctrl+O
Close	
Save	Ctrl+S
Save As...	
Save All	
Find File...	
Summary Info...	
Templates...	
Page Setup...	
Print Preview	
Print...	Ctrl+P
1 2FIG7-8.DOC	
2 MARKETRP.DOC	
3 2FIG6-3.DOC	
4 2FIG6-1.DOC	
Exit	

3 Select a file name from the list box, or type in the name of the file you want to open.

4 If desired, select from file type, directory, or drive options.

5 Click on **OK** or press **Enter**.

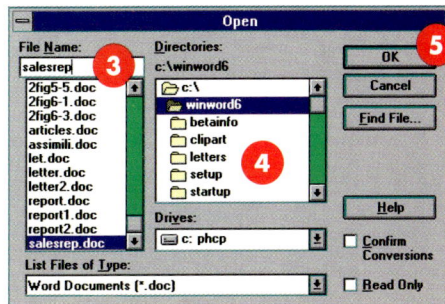

Open

File Name: salesrep

2fig5-5.doc
2fig6-1.doc
2fig6-3.doc
articles.doc
assimili.doc
let.doc
letter.doc
letter2.doc
report.doc
report1.doc
report2.doc
salesrep.doc

Directories: c:\winword6

c:\
winword6
betainfo
clipart
letters
setup
startup

Drives: c: phcp

List Files of Type: Word Documents (*.doc)

OK
Cancel
Find File...
Help

Confirm Conversions
Read Only

TIP

Opening a New Document To open a new document in which to type, use the **N**ew command. Click on **F**ile or press **Alt+F**. Click on **N**ew or press **N**. Then click on **OK** or press **Enter**. A new document will appear in your window. You can also click on the **New Document** button located on the Standard toolbar.

CLOSING A DOCUMENT

Why Close a Document?

When you are finished working on a document you should close it. Closing a document does not exit the Word for Windows program; it just gets one particular document off your screen so you will have more room to work on other documents.

Closing a Document

1 Click on **File** or press **Alt+F**.

2 Click on **Close** or press **C**.

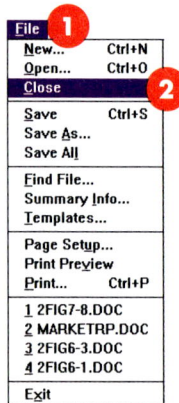

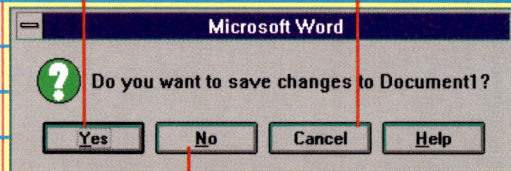

FINDING AND REPLACING TEXT

Why Find and Replace Text?

When working with documents, sometimes you may need to locate a particular word or phrase and replace it with something else. Word for Windows features a convenient way of searching through your text, without scrolling endlessly and reading every paragraph. The **F**ind command and the **R**eplace command can make your search relatively painless.

The Find command, found in the **E**dit menu, quickly locates words or phrases. You can control how the search is conducted, whether Word looks for upper- or lowercase letters, or even what fonts the search includes. There are pull-down lists in the Find dialog box that provide options for your search.

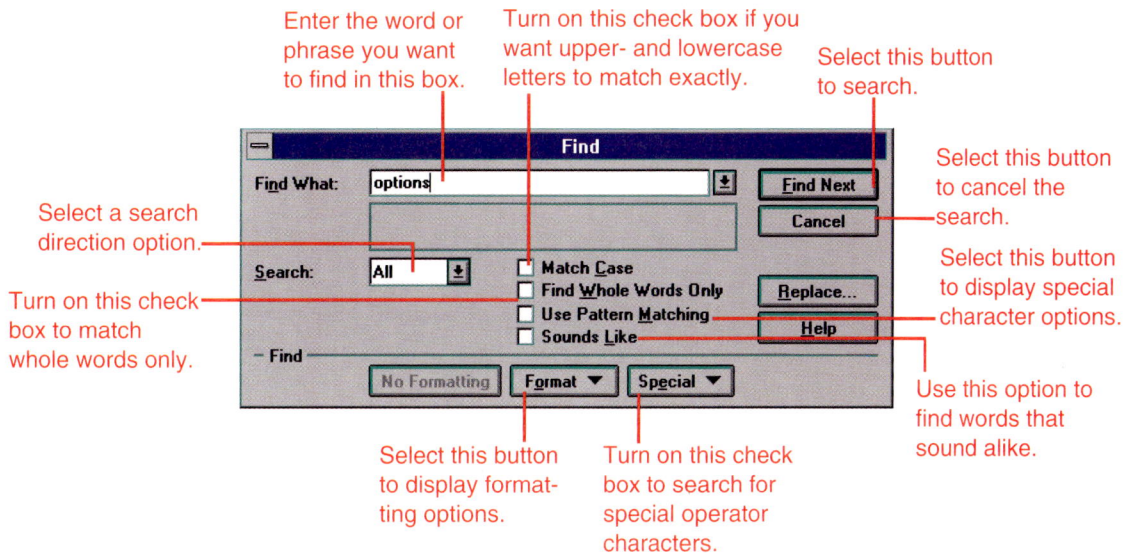

Enter the word or phrase you want to find in this box.

Turn on this check box if you want upper- and lowercase letters to match exactly.

Select this button to search.

Select this button to cancel the search.

Select this button to display special character options.

Select a search direction option.

Turn on this check box to match whole words only.

Use this option to find words that sound alike.

Select this button to display formatting options.

Turn on this check box to search for special operator characters.

LEARNING THE LINGO

Whole Words Only: Only whole words will be found. For example, if you are searching for "and," Word for Windows will not consider the word "band" to be a match.

Match Case: Word for Windows matches upper- and lowercase letters. For example, "Sales" will not match "sales" or "SALES."

FINDING AND REPLACING TEXT

The Replace command not only finds words or phrases, but also replaces them with new text. You can control whether a single text entry is replaced, or every occurrence in the entire document. Use the pull-down lists in the Replace dialog box to select options.

Enter the text you want replaced here.

Turn on this check box to match upper- and lowercase letters.

Enter the replacement text here.

Select a search direction option.

Turn on this check box to find and replace whole words only.

Find the next occurrence of the text.

Replace the current occurrence of the text.

Replace all occurrences of the text in the entire document.

Turn on this check box to search for special operator characters.

Use this option to find words that sound alike.

Select this button to display formatting options.

Select this button to display special character options.

Replace

Find What: options

Replace With: features

Search: All

☐ Match Case
☐ Find Whole Words Only
☐ Use Pattern Matching
☐ Sounds Like

Find Next
Cancel
Replace
Replace All
Help

Replace

No Formatting   Format ▼   Special ▼

TIP

Search and Replace Tip   If the search reaches the end of the document, Word will ask you if you want to continue searching at the beginning of the document. If you select **Y**es, the search will continue until it reaches the place where it started.

TIP

Not Found   If Word cannot find the text, it displays the message **The search text is not found**. If you feel sure that the text is in the document, check the spelling of the text you entered in the Fi**n**d What box and the setting of the Match **W**hole Words Only and Match **C**ase options.

Finding Text

1 Click on Edit or press **Alt+E**.

2 Click on Find or press **F**.

3 Enter the word or phrase for which you want to search.

4 Select any options you want to use in your search.

5 Click Find Next or press **Enter** to begin your search.

6 Word highlights the first occurrence of the text. Click Find Next or press **Enter** to find the next occurrence.

7 Click on **Cancel** or press **Esc** to exit the dialog box.

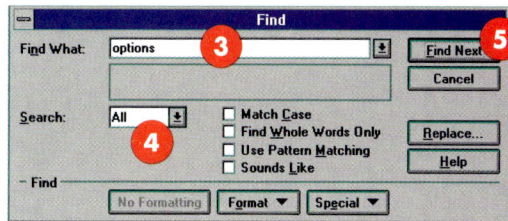

The found word is highlighted in the text block.

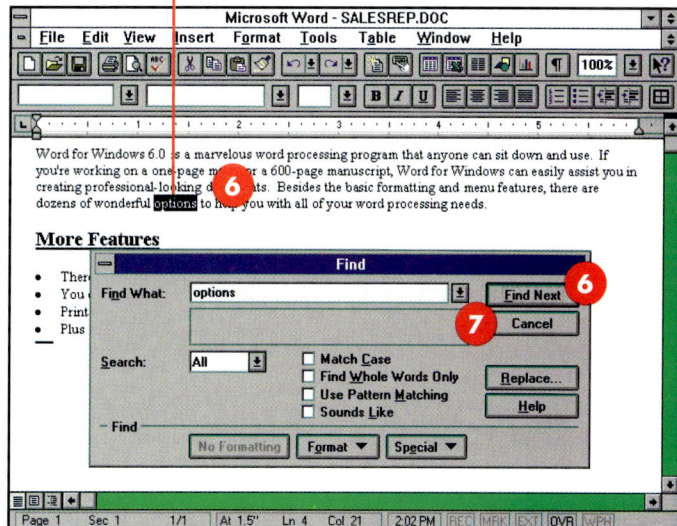

Word for Windows 6.0 is a marvelous word processing program that anyone can sit down and use. If you're working on a one-page memo or a 600-page manuscript, Word for Windows can easily assist you in creating professional-looking documents. Besides the basic formatting and menu features, there are dozens of wonderful options to help you with all of your word processing needs.

More Features

Finding and Replacing Text

1 Click on **E**dit or press **Alt+E**.

2 Click on **Re**place or press **E**.

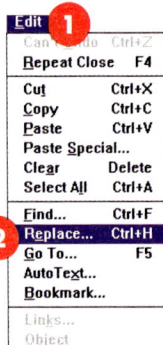

3 Enter the word or phrase for which you want to search.

4 Enter the replacement text.

5 Select any options you want to use in your search.

6 Click on the command buttons to begin your search and replace.

7 Click on **Cancel** or press **Esc** to exit the dialog box.

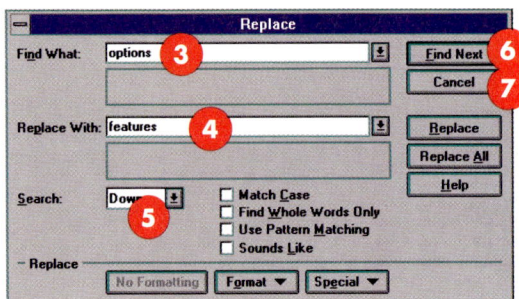

TIP

Search and Delete   To delete all occurrences of the specified text in your document, use the **E**dit

Replace command but leave the Re**p**lace With box empty.

ZOOMING IN AND OUT

What Is a Zoom?

The **Zoom** feature allows you to magnify portions of your document. You can zoom in for a closer look at your document's details (based on percentages of actual size). Or you can zoom out to see the entire document page.

Zooming in and out is a handy way of previewing what your document will look like before it's printed. It also helps you gauge how the layout looks, and check to see if everything is placed where you want it.

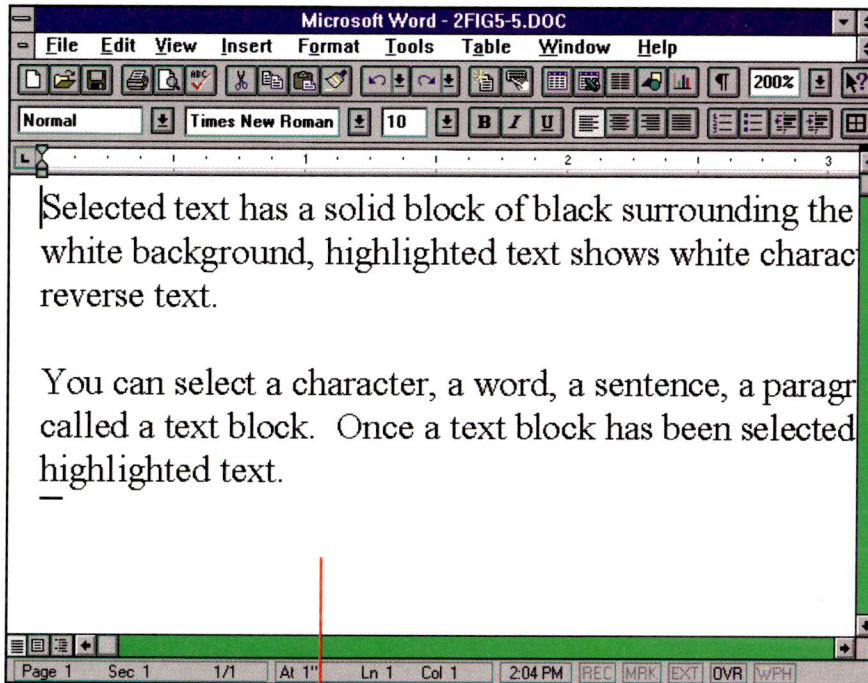

A 200% zoom lets you see the text up close.

LEARNING THE LINGO

Zoom: To magnify a portion of a document.

ZOOMING IN AND OUT

Zooming

1 Click View or press **Alt+V**.

2 Click on Zoom or press **Z**.

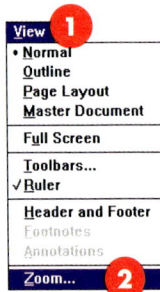

3 Select the perspective in which you want to see the document.

4 Check the view in the Preview window.

5 Click on **OK** or press **Enter**.

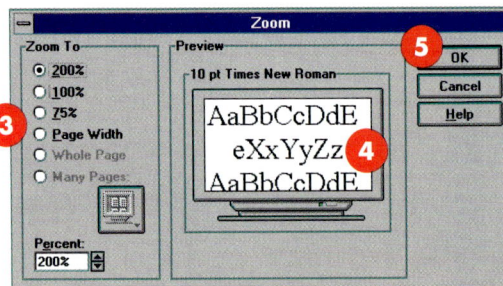

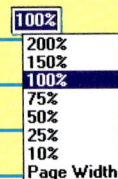

TIP

Quick Zoom Use the **Scale View** drop-down list on the Standard toolbar to zoom in or out quickly. Just click the arrow to display the list, or click inside the box and type in a specific zoom percentage.

100%
200%
150%
100%
75%
50%
25%
10%
Page Width

WORKING WITH MULTIPLE DOCUMENTS

Why Work with Multiple Documents?

A great advantage of Word for Windows 6.0 is the ability to work with more than one document at a time. You can open and work on a new file while the previous file you were using is still open. This makes moving and copying text from one file to another a very simple operation.

Best of all, you can display your multiple documents on one screen, all at the same time. This allows you to see into several documents at once. The document you are currently working in has a highlighted title bar, indicating the window is *active*. The **W**indow menu has an **A**rrange All option that you can use to display your multiple documents.

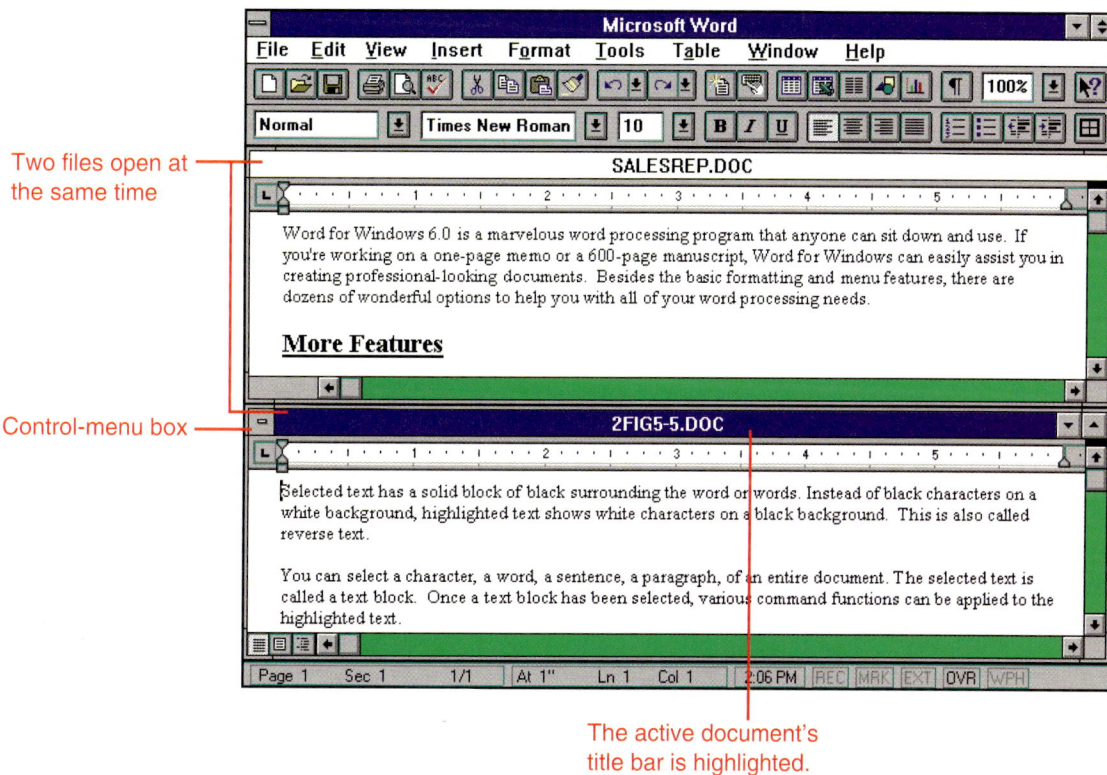

Two files open at the same time

Control-menu box

The active document's title bar is highlighted.

LEARNING THE LINGO

Active document: The document you are working on currently, which is indicated by a highlighted title bar. When more than one document is opened, you can work on only one document at a time.

WORKING WITH MULTIPLE DOCUMENTS

Arranging Multiple Documents on Your Screen

1 Make sure two document files are opened. Click on **Window** or press **Alt+W**.

2 Click on **Arrange All** or press **A**.

```
Window          1
New Window
Arrange All     2
Split
1 2FIG5-5.DOC
√2 SALESREP.DOC
```

QUICK REFRESHER

To close a document at any time:

1. Click on **File** or press **Alt+F**.

2. Click on **Close** or press **C**.

You can also double-click on the document's Control-menu box to close the document.

QUICK REFRESHER

To copy or move text between windows, select the text to be copied or moved. Press **Ctrl+C** to copy; press **Ctrl+X** to cut and move. Move the cursor to the document into which you want to insert the text. Press **Ctrl+V**. You can also use the Cut, Copy, and Paste tools from the Standard toolbar.

TIP

Switcheroo   When working with several open documents that are not all displayed on-screen at the same time, you can use the **W**indow menu to easily switch from one open document window to another.

1. Click on **Window** or press **Alt+W**.

2. At the bottom of the menu is a list of open files. A check mark denotes which file is the active document. To switch from one to another, click on the file name (or highlight it with the arrow keys and press **Enter**).

```
Window
New Window
Arrange All
Split
1 2FIG5-5.DOC
√2 SALESREP.DOC
```

TIP

Changing Active Windows and Moving Them Around You can make a window active by clicking anywhere inside of the window. Remember, the active window will always have a highlighted title bar. You can also move your multiple windows around on-screen. Just move the mouse pointer to the title bar of the window you want to move, press the left mouse button, and drag the window to a new position. Release the button and you've relocated your window!

To adjust the edges of the window, move the mouse pointer over a border edge (your mouse pointer will change to a two-headed arrow), press the mouse button, and drag the border to a new size.

QUICK REFRESHER

When you open another file without closing the document you were working with, the new file appears in your document window. The old file is there, too—you just can't see it.

To open another file on top of your current file, follow these steps:

1. With a document open in the document window, click on **F**ile or press **Alt+F**.

2. Click on **O**pen or press **O**.

3. The Open File dialog box will appear. Select another file to open, and then click on **OK** or press **Enter**.

Creating, Editing, Saving, and Printing Documents

PRINTING A DOCUMENT

When Can a Document Be Printed?

You can print a document at any time, but ordinarily you'll want to print it after you've completed work on it. It's a good idea to preview your document before you print it out, so you can make sure everything looks the way you want it to. Take a look at the "Using Print Preview" task in this section.

When you're finally ready to print, use the **P**rint command found in the **F**ile menu. The Print dialog box will appear, offering you many printing options. You can control how many copies are printed, the print quality, and more.

Use the drop-down list to select the type of information you want to print. Leave this list set to document to print the document.

Displays the name of the active printer.

To print more than one copy, select from this box. Choose the up or down arrow, or type a value.

Use these options to select what part of the document to print.

Select OK to print the document.

Additional printing options

Select to change printers.

Print

Printer: HP LaserJet III on LPT1:

Print What: Document

Copies: 1

Page Range
- ◉ All
- ○ Current Page   ○ Selection
- ○ Pages:

Enter page numbers and/or page ranges separated by commas. For example, 1,3,5-12

Print: All Pages in Range

OK
Cancel
Options...
Printer...
Help

☐ Print to File
☒ Collate Copies

Use this drop-down list to select the order in which you want the pages printed.

TIP

Printing Tip   For printing to work properly, your system must have a printer connected to it. The printer must be turned on, loaded with paper, and set to "on-line."

Printing a Document

1 Click on **F**ile or press **Alt+F**.

2 Click on **P**rint or press **P**.

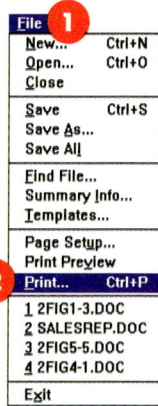

3 Change printing options (as desired) in the Print dialog box.

4 When you are ready to print, click on **OK** or press **Enter**.

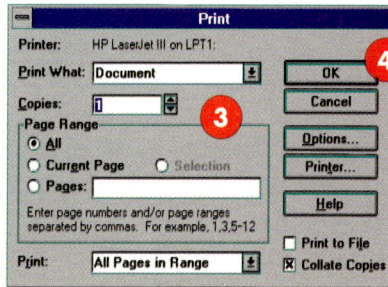

TIP

Quick Print For a faster way of printing, click on the **Print** button on the Standard toolbar.

TIP

Using Page Setup The Page Setup options, located on the **F**ile menu, allow you to change paper size, margins, orientation, and more. Turn to the "Using Page Setup" task in Part 3 for more information.

USING PRINT PREVIEW

Why Use Print Preview?

Print Preview shows you on-screen exactly how your document will look when it is printed. You can view one or two entire pages on-screen at the same time, which lets you evaluate the appearance of margins and page breaks. You can even edit a document's text or formatting in Print Preview, as well as change margin settings.

To use Print Preview, select Print Preview from the **F**ile menu. The page containing the insertion point will be displayed.

Returns the window to whole page view.

Shows or hides the Ruler.

Use this tool to fit document on fewer pages.

Zooms in or out to magnify portions of the document.

Scales the editing view by percentages.

Toggle window to an up-close full-page view.

Exits Print Preview.

Prints the document.

Use to set page margins.

Shows multiple pages.

Use this ruler to change top and bottom margins.

Drag to change left or right margins.

Use the scroll bar to view other parts of the document or other pages.

Click outside the page to update new margin settings.

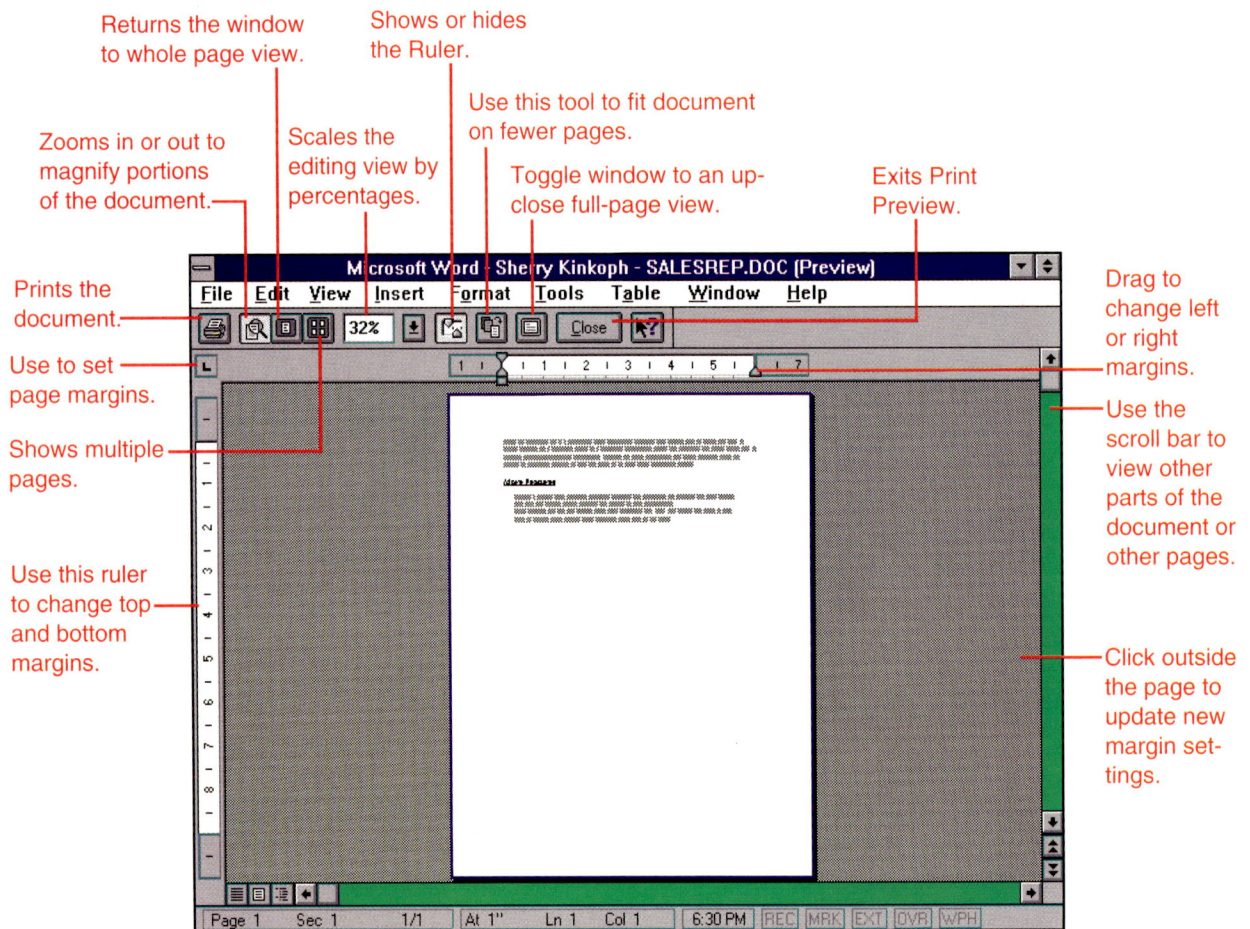

Microsoft Word - Sherry Kinkoph - SALESREP.DOC [Preview]

File   Edit   View   Insert   Format   Tools   Table   Window   Help

32%   Close

Page 1   Sec 1   1/1   At 1"   Ln 1   Col 1   6:30 PM   REC   MRK   EXT   OVR   WPH

Using Print Preview

1 Click on File or press **Alt+F**.

2 Click on Print Preview or press **V**.

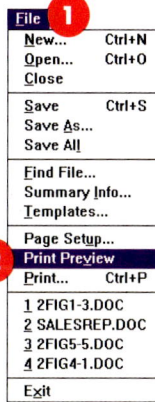

3 Change options, if desired.

4 Click on **Close** to exit Print Preview.

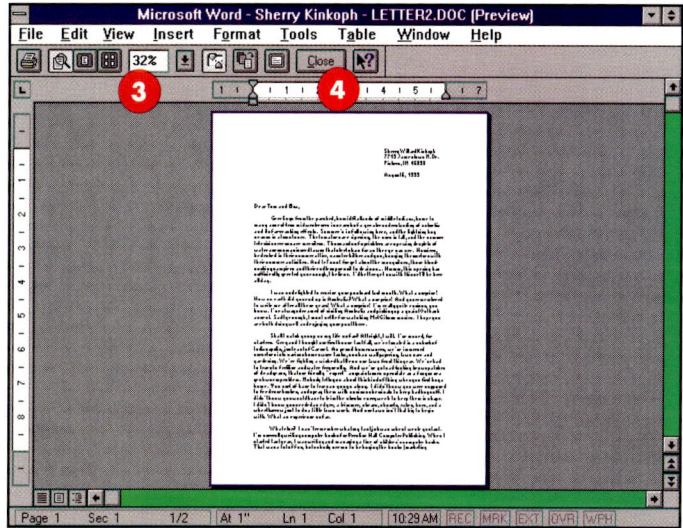

TIP

Quick Print You can print your document from the Print Preview screen. Just click the **Print** button on the Standard toolbar. You can also pull down the **F**ile menu and select **P**rint or press **P**.

67

PART 3

Formatting Your Document

In this section, you will learn how to control the formatting, or appearance, of your documents. These tasks will help you to create attractive and effective documents.

- Formatting Characters
- Formatting Paragraphs
- Working with the Ruler
- Setting Tabs
- Setting Margins
- Using Page Setup
- Indenting Text
- Aligning Text

FORMATTING CHARACTERS

Why Format Characters?

Formatting characters changes the font, size, and style (underline, italics, and so on) of the letters. You use character formatting to emphasize certain parts of your document and to improve its appearance. You can specify character formatting before you enter text; then as you type, the new text appears in the selected character style. You can also select a block of existing text and change its formatting.

You can set character formatting options with the Font command from the Format menu. This displays the Font dialog box. Within the Font dialog box are two tabs, or parts of the dialog box that look like folders: Font and Character Spacing. Clicking on the tab, or pressing Alt plus the selection letter, brings a folder to the front of the dialog box. Both tabs have formatting options and command buttons from which to choose.

Scroll along this list to select a font style.

Scroll along this list to select a font.

Select an underline style: None, Single, Words Only, Double, or Dotted.

Turn on these check boxes to select Effects options.

Click on the Character Spacing tab or press Alt+R to reveal character spacing commands.

Scroll along this list or type in the box to specify the size of letters in points.

Choose a text color with this drop-down list.

Look here to see how the formatting options will appear.

Click on the Font tab or press Alt+N to reveal Font commands.

Specify spacing between characters with the Spacing option.

Specify vertical positioning (also called leading in typesetting terminology) of characters with the Positioning option.

Automatically changes character spacing based on font.

Formatting Characters

1 Move the cursor to where you want new formatting to appear, or select the text whose format you want to change.

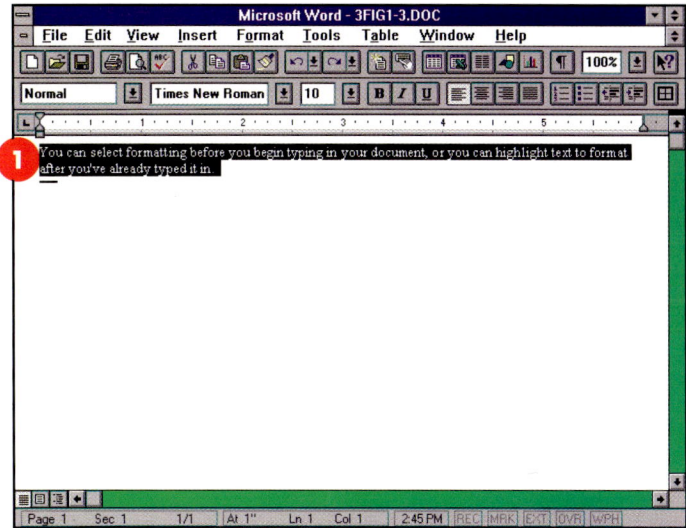

2 Click on Format or press **Alt+O**.

3 Click on Font or press **F**.

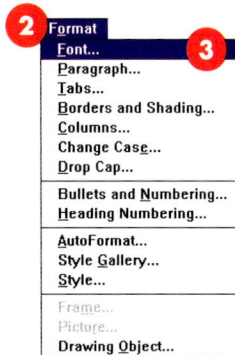

4 If the Font tab is not at the front of the dialog box, click the tab name or press **Alt+N**.

5 Select the desired character formatting options from the Font tab.

6 Click on the Character Spacing tab or press **Alt+R** to reveal the character spacing commands.

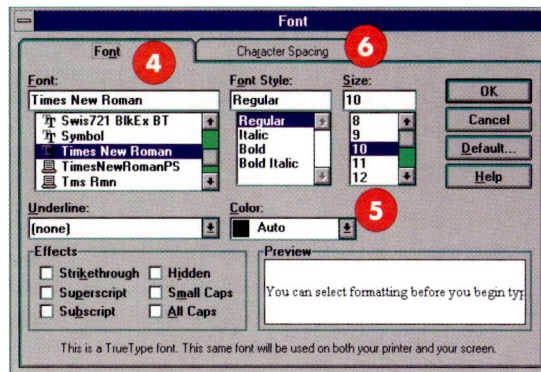

71

Formatting Your Document

FORMATTING CHARACTERS

7 Select the desired character spacing options.

8 Click **OK** or press **Enter**.

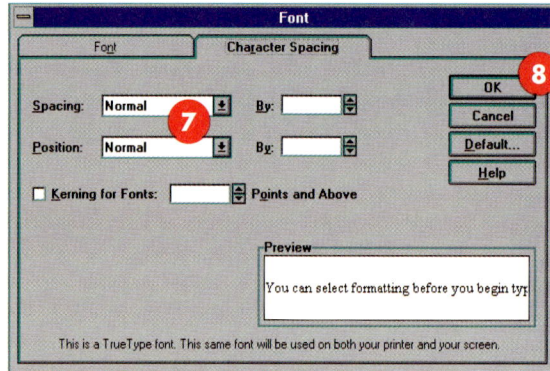

Here are some keyboard shortcuts for applying character formatting to selected text or text you are typing:

Bold	`CTRL` + `B`
Italic	`CTRL` + `I`
Underline	`CTRL` + `U`
No special formatting (turns all formatting off)	`CTRL` + `SPACE`

TIP

Formatting Toolbar Shortcuts   You can quickly select character formatting using the Formatting toolbar. The toolbar displays the font name and size for the text where the cursor is located. If the text is Bold, Italic, or Underlined, the corresponding button appears to be pressed.

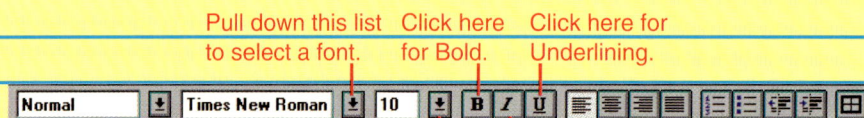

Pull down this list to select a font.   Click here for Bold.   Click here for Underlining.

| Normal | Times New Roman | 10 | **B** *I* U̲ | |

Pull down this list or type in a value to select a point size.   Click here for Italics.

72

Exercise

Enter the text shown in this figure and practice changing the character formatting.

1 Select the first line and make it 18-point bold.

2 Select the second line and underline it.

3 Select the word **Congratulations!** and make it italic.

```
Microsoft Word - 3FIG1-8.DOC
File  Edit  View  Insert  Format  Tools  Table  Window  Help

Normal    Times New Roman   10   B  I  U

To:        All Employees

From:    Lisa Jamison, CEO

Congratulations!  We've achieved all of our sales objectives for the fourth quarter.  Thanks to all of your
efforts and involvement, we've reached our yearly goal as of 5:00 p.m. Wednesday.  We'll send out a
memo detailing this quarter's accomplishments sometime early next week.

Page 1    Sec 1    1/1    At 2.1"    Ln 7    Col 72    2:47 PM   REC MRK EXT OVR WPH
```

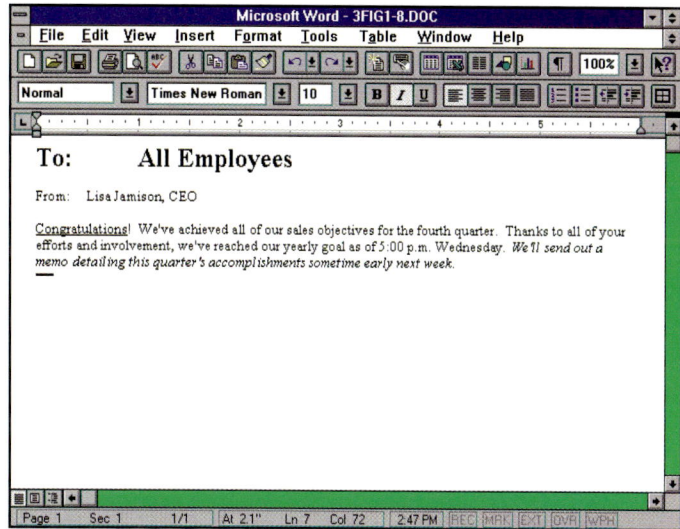

QUICK REFRESHER

Selecting text with the mouse

Position the I-beam at the start of the text, press and hold the left mouse button, drag the highlight to the end of the text, and release the mouse button.

Selecting text with the keyboard

Position the insertion point at the start of the text, press and hold **Shift**, and use the arrow keys to stretch the highlight.

Formatting Your Document

FORMATTING PARAGRAPHS

Why Format Paragraphs?

Paragraph formatting controls the appearance of entire paragraphs, such as the indentation, line spacing, and alignment. (Remember that you mark the end of a paragraph, and the start of the next paragraph, by pressing Enter.)

To set paragraph formatting, select **P**aragraph from the **F**ormat menu. This displays the Paragraph dialog box. Within the Paragraph dialog box are two tabs, or parts of the dialog box that look like folders: **I**ndents and Spacing and Text **F**low. Clicking on the tab, or pressing Alt plus the selection letter, will bring a folder to the front of the dialog box. Both tabs have formatting options and command buttons from which to choose.

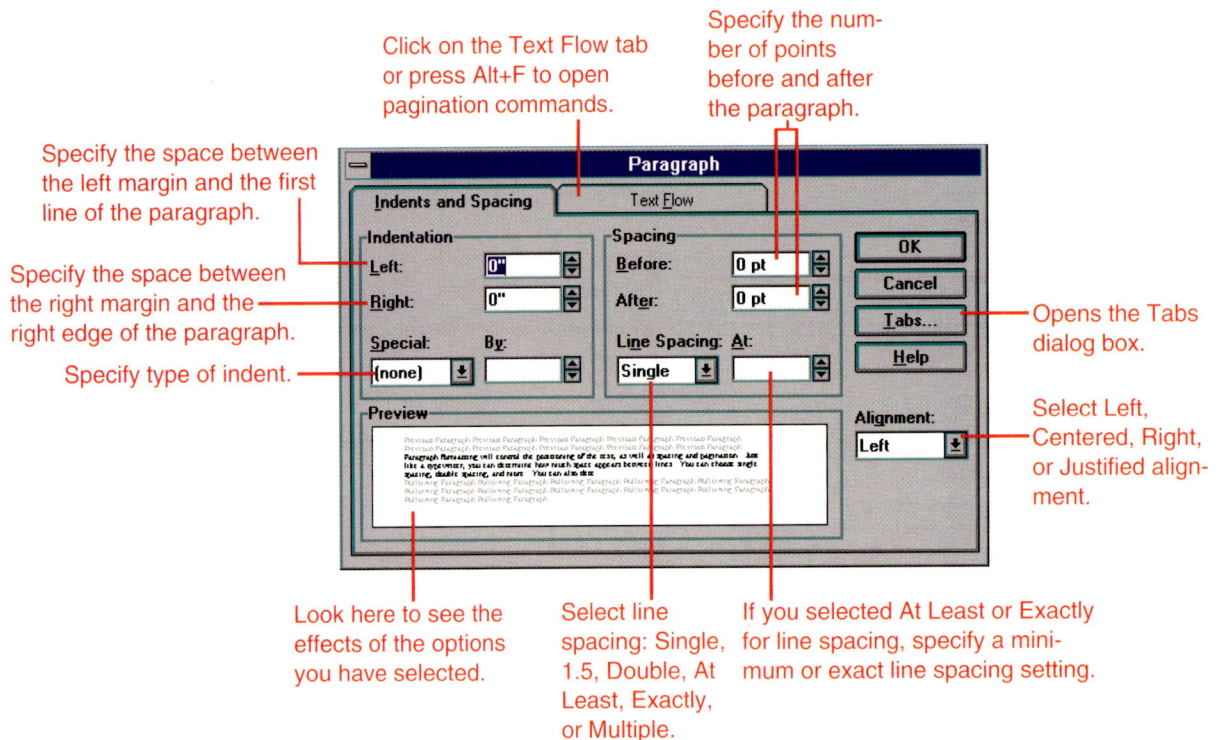

Click on the Text Flow tab or press Alt+F to open pagination commands.

Specify the number of points before and after the paragraph.

Specify the space between the left margin and the first line of the paragraph.

Specify the space between the right margin and the right edge of the paragraph.

Specify type of indent.

Opens the Tabs dialog box.

Select Left, Centered, Right, or Justified alignment.

Look here to see the effects of the options you have selected.

Select line spacing: Single, 1.5, Double, At Least, Exactly, or Multiple.

If you selected At Least or Exactly for line spacing, specify a minimum or exact line spacing setting.

LEARNING THE LINGO

Alignment: Positioning of text between the left and right margins. Also known as *justification*.

Spacing: The amount of space between characters or between lines.

Pagination: The manner in which document pages are layed out from page to page—how paragraphs flow, where page breaks occur, and so on.

Indent: To shift a line of text away from the left or right margins.

Click on the Indents and Spacing tab or press Alt+I to open the alignment and spacing commands.

Turn this check box on to ensure that the specified paragraph will be on the same page as the next paragraph.

Turn this check box on to control the appearance of a single word positioned at the end of a paragraph.

Turn this check box on to ensure that the entire paragraph will be printed on the same page.

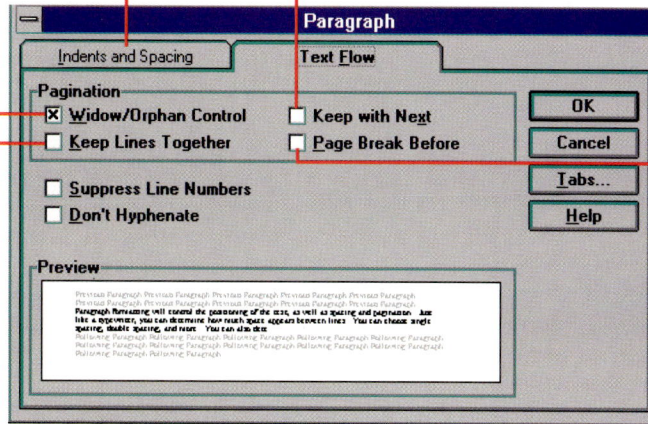

Turn this check box on to have the paragraph appear at the top of a new page.

Formatting Paragraphs

1 Select the paragraphs to format if you want to format more than one. For a single paragraph, place the cursor anywhere in the paragraph. To start a new paragraph, place the cursor on a blank line.

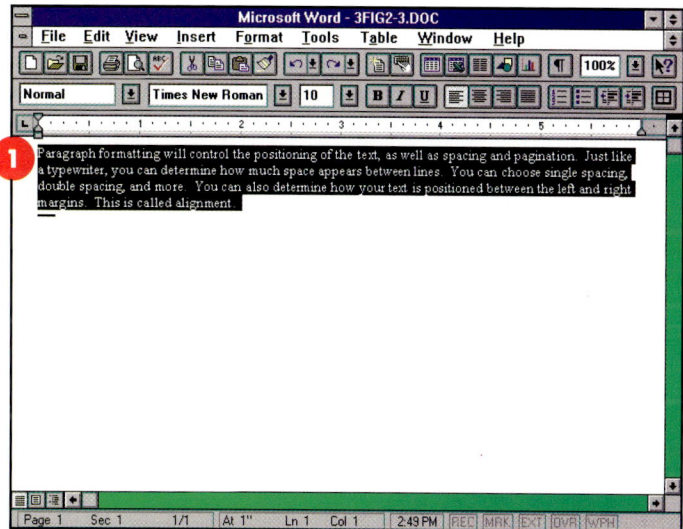

2 Click on **F**ormat or press **Alt+O**.

3 Click on **P**aragraph or press **P**.

Formatting Your Document

FORMATTING PARAGRAPHS

4 If the Indents and Spacing tab is not at the front of the dialog box, click the tab name or press **Alt+I**.

5 Select the formatting options you want from the Indents and Spacing tab.

6 Click on the Text Flow tab or press **Alt+F** to open the pagination commands.

7 Select the pagination options you want to use from the Text Flow tab.

8 Click on **OK**, or press **Enter**.

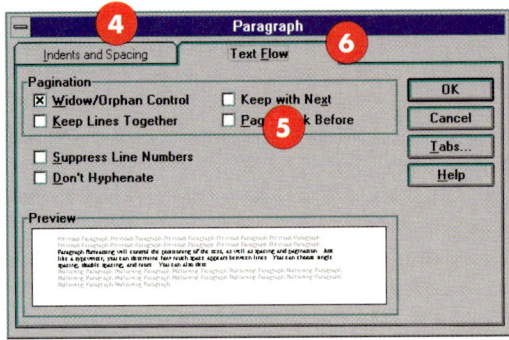

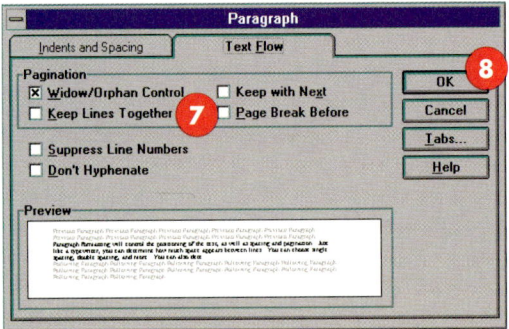

TIP

Formatting Toolbar Shortcuts   You can quickly select paragraph formatting using the Formatting toolbar. The toolbar displays alignment buttons that you can quickly access at the click of a mouse button.

Select the paragraph to be formatted. Then click the appropriate alignment button from the Formatting toolbar.

Click here to undo an indent by one tab stop.

Click here for left alignment.   Click here for right alignment.   Click here to indent one tab stop.

| Normal | Times New Roman | 10 | **B** *I* U |

Click here for centered alignment.   Click here for text that is justified—both left and right alignment.

Exercise

Enter the text shown in this figure and change the paragraph formatting.

1 Set Alignment to Justified for all three paragraphs.

2 Change both the Left and Right indentation of the second paragraph to 1 inch.

3 Change the line spacing to Double for the entire document.

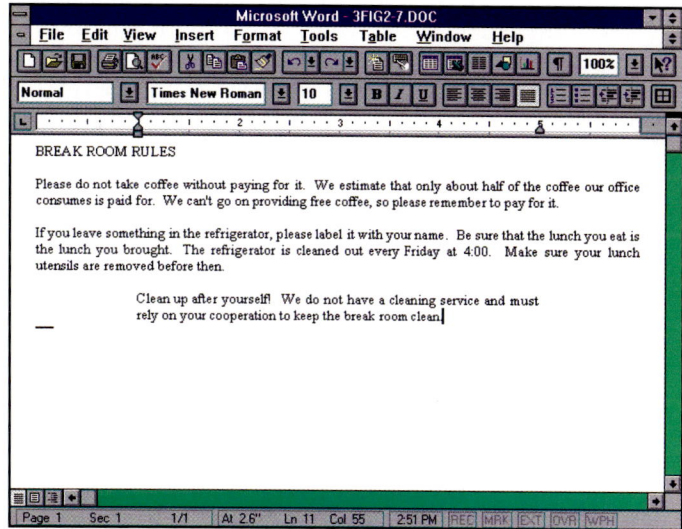

Microsoft Word - 3FIG2-7.DOC

File Edit View Insert Format Tools Table Window Help

Normal   Times New Roman   10   B I U

BREAK ROOM RULES

Please do not take coffee without paying for it. We estimate that only about half of the coffee our office consumes is paid for. We can't go on providing free coffee, so please remember to pay for it.

If you leave something in the refrigerator, please label it with your name. Be sure that the lunch you eat is the lunch you brought. The refrigerator is cleaned out every Friday at 4:00. Make sure your lunch utensils are removed before then.

Clean up after yourself! We do not have a cleaning service and must rely on your cooperation to keep the break room clean.

Page 1   Sec 1   1/1   At 2.6"   Ln 11   Col 55   2:51 PM   REC MRK EXT OVR WPH

Formatting Your Document

WORKING WITH THE RULER

What Does the Ruler Do?

The Ruler can help you set margins and tabs, and set up tables and columns in your document. When you start Word for Windows 6.0, the Ruler automatically appears beneath the Formatting toolbar. To learn how to use the Ruler, turn to the "Setting Tabs" and "Setting Margins" tasks later in this section.

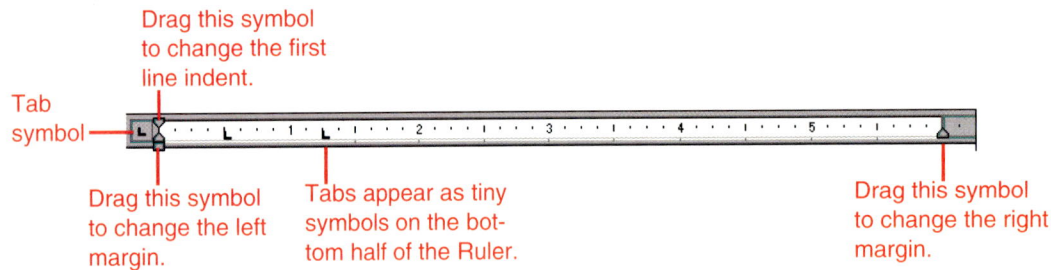

Drag this symbol
to change the first
line indent.

Tab
symbol

Drag this symbol
to change the left
margin.

Tabs appear as tiny
symbols on the bot-
tom half of the Ruler.

Drag this symbol
to change the right
margin.

Displaying and Hiding the Ruler

1 To display or hide the Ruler, click on **View** or press **Alt+V**.

2 Click on **Ruler** or press **R**. A check mark next to the command indicates the Ruler will be displayed. If there is no check mark, the Ruler will be hidden.

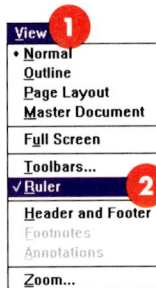

View **1**
• **N**ormal
Outline
Page Layout
Master Document
F**u**ll Screen
Toolbars...
√ **R**uler **2**
Header and Footer
F**o**otnotes
A**n**notations
Zoom...

LEARNING THE LINGO

Margin: The space between your text and the outer edge of your page.

Tab: A keystroke that moves text to a specified point in your document. Tabs are used to align text.

TIP

Double-Click Shortcuts Double-click the mouse button on the top half of the Ruler to display the Page Setup dialog box. Double-click on the bottom half of the Ruler to display the Tabs dialog box.

What Are Tabs?

Tab stops are specific locations on a line of text, defined by Word or by you, that allow you to align entries in a column or to indent text. Whenever you press the Tab key, the insertion point and any text to the right of it move over to the next tab stop.

Word provides default tab stops that are spaced one-half inch apart. You can add new tab stops, change the position of existing tab stops, or change tab stop alignment. To set or modify tab stops, issue the **T**abs command on the F**o**rmat menu to display the Tabs dialog box.

Select the desired tab alignment.

Specify a new spacing for the default tab stops with this box.

Clears all tabs listed in the Tab Stops to be Cleared List and closes the dialog box.

Type in the distance in inches of the new tab stop from the left margin.

If the current paragraph has any custom tabs, they are listed here. Select one to modify or delete.

Sets a tab at the position entered in the Tab Stop Position box.

Adds the selected tab stop to the Tab Stops to Be Cleared list.

Tab stops to be cleared are listed here.

Select the desired tab leader character.

Clears all tab stops.

Tab Symbols	Description
⌐	**Left tab:** The left edge of text aligns at the tab stop.
⌐	**Right tab:** The right edge of text aligns at the tab stop.
⊥	**Center tab:** Text is centered at the tab stop.
⊥.	**Decimal tab:** The decimal points align at the tab stop.

SETTING TABS

Setting Tab Stops

1 Move the cursor to where you want the new tab stop to take effect, or select paragraphs for the new tab stop to affect.

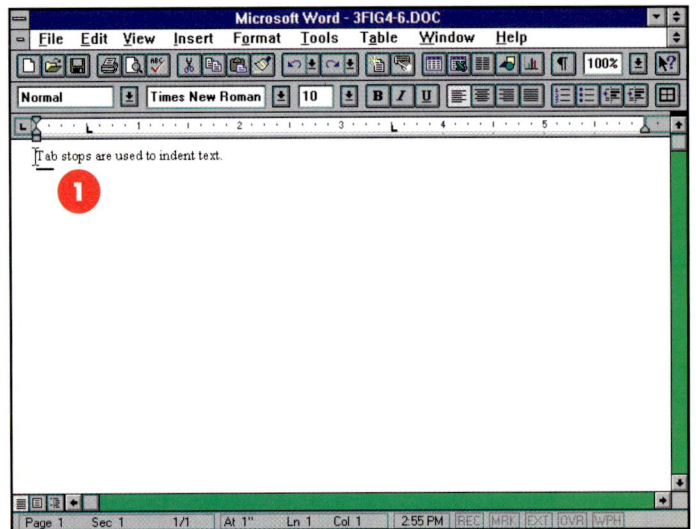

2 Click on **F**ormat or press **Alt+O**.

3 Click on **T**abs or press **T**.

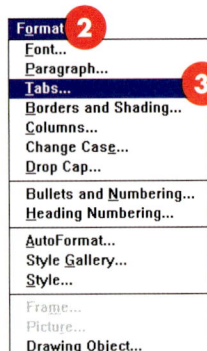

4 Enter the new tab stop position in inches.

5 Specify a new spacing for the default tab stops, if desired.

6 Select alignment and leader options.

7 Click on **S**et or press **Alt+S** to set the new tab stop.

8 Click on **OK** or press **Enter** to close the dialog box.

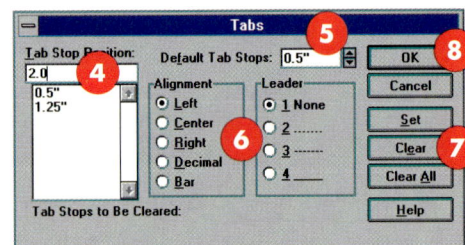

Exercise

Enter the text shown in the figure, indenting the first line of each paragraph one tab stop. Move the insertion point to the start of the document and modify the tab stop settings as directed in the following steps.

1 Change the default tab stop spacing to 1 inch.

2 Insert a custom tab stop at 0.75 inch.

3 Delete the custom tab stop.

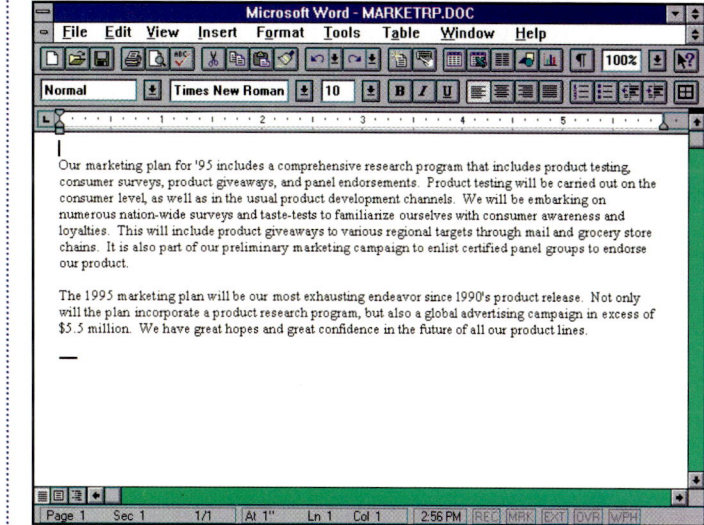

TIP

Tabbing with the Ruler   You can set and clear tabs stops with the Ruler and mouse. If the Ruler is not visible, issue the **V**iew **R**uler command to display it.

To set a new tab stop, click the desired position on the lower half of the Ruler.

Choose the tab type symbol you want to use by clicking here.

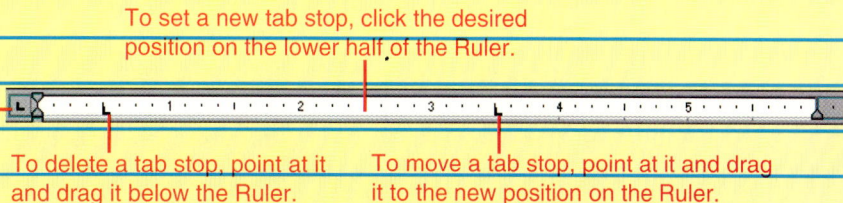

To delete a tab stop, point at it and drag it below the Ruler.

To move a tab stop, point at it and drag it to the new position on the Ruler.

Tab stops apply to any paragraphs you have selected. Otherwise, they apply from the insertion point onward.

TIP

What Are Leader Characters?   Leader characters are characters, such as a hyphen or a dot, that fill the tab space between words. Leader characters can be set in the Tab dialog box. Just select the appropriate style to use.

Leader
- ● **1** None
- ○ **2** ....
- ○ **3** -------
- ○ **4** ____

Formatting Your Document

SETTING MARGINS

What Are Margins?

Margins are the space between your text and the edges of the paper. Each page has four margins: Top, Bottom, Left, and Right.

Word's default margins are fine for most situations, but you can change them as needed for all or part of a document. For example, if you're writing a letter that almost fits on one page, you may be able to make it fit by decreasing all four margin settings by a fraction of an inch. Or, if you're writing a very short letter, you can make it seem more substantial by increasing all four margins by a half-inch or so.

To change page margins, choose Page Setup from the File menu to display the Page Setup dialog box. Within the Page Setup dialog box are four tabs, or parts of the dialog box that look like folders. One is labeled **Margins**, and that's the one you need to use to change margin settings.

Choose this tab to change page margins.

Look here to see how your settings will appear.

Set the Top margin.
Set the Bottom margin.
Set the Left margin.
Set the Right margin.

Use the Gutter margin to leave space between columns.

Page Setup

| Margins | Paper Size | Paper Source | Layout |

Top: 1"
Bottom: 1"
Left: 1.25"
Right: 1.25"
Gutter: 0"

From Edge
Header: 0.5"
Footer: 0.5"

Preview

OK
Cancel
Default...
Help

Mirror Margins

Apply To: Whole Document

You can make the new margin settings the default for all new documents with this button.

Controls placement of Headers and Footers

Specifies where the new margin settings should apply.

TIP

Ruler Shortcuts   You can change the left and right margins of selected text using the Ruler. On the Ruler, click on the left margin marker to display the margin markers. Drag the left margin marker or the right margin marker to change the margins.

L   1   2   3   4   5

Drag this symbol to change the left margin.

Drag this symbol to change the first line indent.

Drag this symbol to change the right margin.

Changing Page Margins

1 Move the cursor to where you want the new margins to take effect, or select the text you want them to affect.

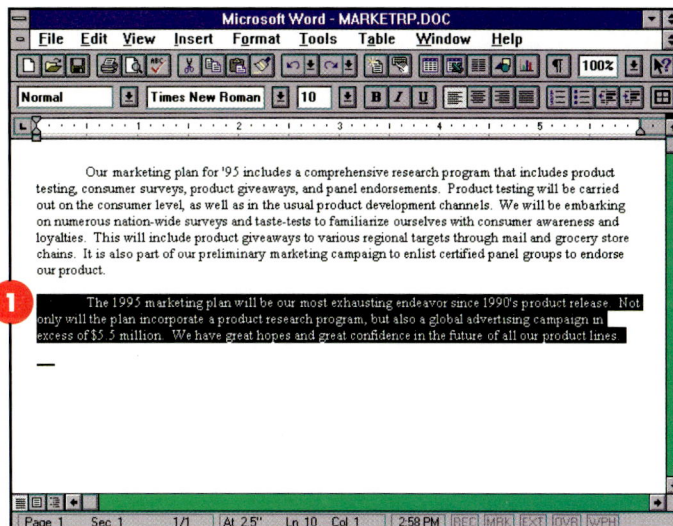

2 Click on **File** or press **Alt+F**.

3 Click on Page Set**u**p or press **U**.

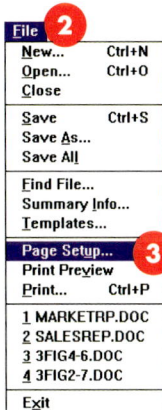

4 If necessary, click the **Margins** tab button to bring the Margins tab to the front of the dialog box.

5 Enter the new values for the margins.

6 Specify the part of the document where you want the new settings to apply.

7 Click on **OK** or press **Enter** to exit the box.

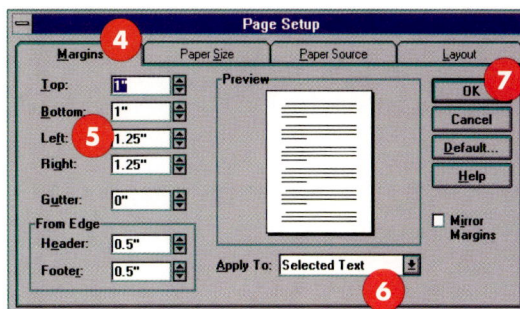

Formatting Your Document

83

SETTING MARGINS

> ## TIP
>
> **When to Use Margins**   When you change the margins, the new settings can be applied to the entire document, can be applied from the location of the insertion point on, or can be applied to a block of selected text only.

What Is Page Setup?

Another part of formatting your document is setting up your page orientation. You must specify the size and orientation of your paper so that Word can print your document properly. Word's default is 8 1/2-by-11-inch paper in portrait orientation, which is fine for most documents. Your printer may offer other size and orientation options.

To specify paper size and orientation, use the Page Set**u**p command found on the **F**ile menu to display the Page Setup dialog box. Within the Page Setup dialog box are four tabs, or parts of the dialog box that look like folders. They are **M**argins (covered in "Setting Margins" earlier in this section), Paper **S**ize, **P**aper Source, and **L**ayout. Each of these tabs has setup options you can use.

Click this tab to bring the Paper Size options to the front of the dialog box.

Look here to see what your page will look like.

Select from predefined paper sizes.

For a custom size, enter the width and height in these boxes or click the arrows to choose values.

Choose either Portrait or Landscape orientation.

Use this button to make the new settings the default for all new documents.

Specify whether the new settings will apply to the entire document or from the insertion point on.

Click this tab to bring the Paper Source options to the front of the dialog box.

Depending on the type of printer, you can change the paper source with the options on this tab.

Formatting Your Document

USING PAGE SETUP

Page Setup

| Margins | Paper Size | Paper Source | Layout |

Click this tab to bring the Layout options to the front of the dialog box.

Select options to affect the layout of the document page with the options on this tab.

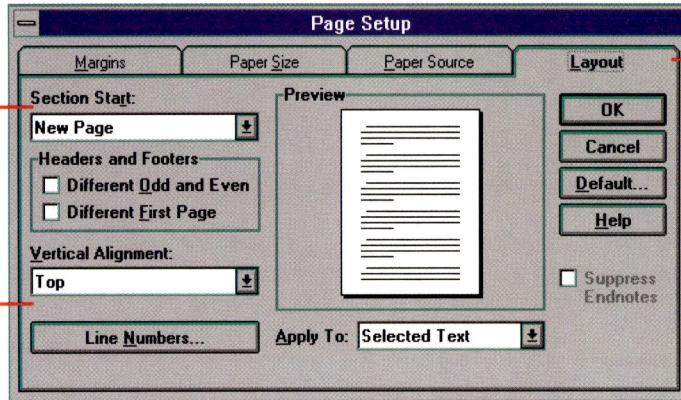

Section Start:
New Page

Headers and Footers
- [ ] Different Odd and Even
- [ ] Different First Page

Vertical Alignment:
Top

Preview

OK
Cancel
Default...
Help

[ ] Suppress Endnotes

Line Numbers...   Apply To: Selected Text

Changing Paper Size and Orientation

1 Click on **File** or press **Alt+F**.

2 Click on Page Set**u**p or press **U**.

File
New...	Ctrl+N
Open...	Ctrl+O
Close	
Save	Ctrl+S
Save As...	
Save All	
Find File...	
Summary Info...	
Templates...	
Page Setup...	
Print Preview	
Print...	Ctrl+P
1 MARKETRP.DOC	
2 SALESREP.DOC	
3 3FIG4-6.DOC	
4 3FIG2-7.DOC	
Exit	

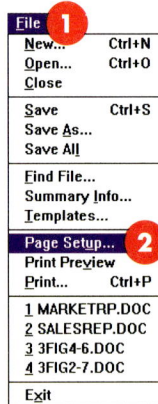

3 Click the various tabs to open the specific setup options you need to select.

4 Select the desired size and orientation options.

5 Specify the part of the document where you want the new settings to apply.

6 Click on **OK** or press **Enter**.

Page Setup

| Margins | Paper Size | Paper Source | Layout |

Paper Size :
Letter 8 ½ x 11 in

Width: 8.5"
Height: 11"

Orientation
- (•) Portrait
- ( ) Landscape

Preview

OK
Cancel
Default...
Help

Apply To: Selected Text

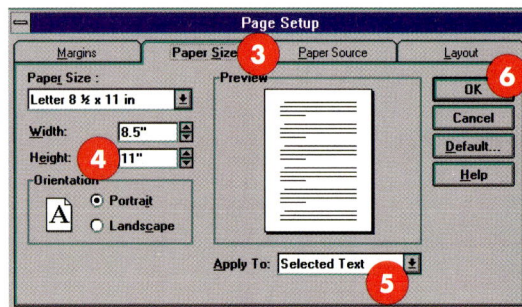

LEARNING THE LINGO

Portrait orientation: Lines of text are parallel to the paper's short edge.

Landscape orientation: Lines of text are parallel to the paper's long edge.

INDENTING TEXT

Why Indent Text?

Indents are used to place extra distance between text and margins. Indents can set off a block of text within your document, draw attention to special paragraphs for emphasis, and improve the overall look of your document.

You can indent a line, a block of text, a paragraph, or an entire document. Each time you indent, text moves over by one tab stop. You can indent before you start typing, or after text is entered.

A First Line indent will shift the first line in a paragraph, but leave the rest of the paragraph intact at its original position.

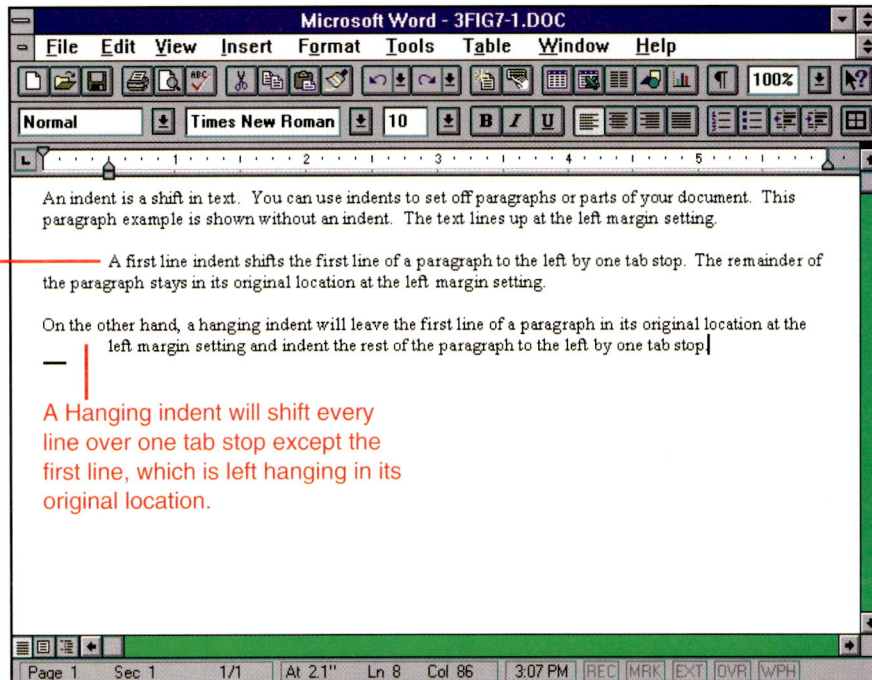

A Hanging indent will shift every line over one tab stop except the first line, which is left hanging in its original location.

Microsoft Word - 3FIG7-1.DOC

File Edit View Insert Format Tools Table Window Help

Normal   Times New Roman   10   **B** *I* <u>U</u>

An indent is a shift in text. You can use indents to set off paragraphs or parts of your document. This paragraph example is shown without an indent. The text lines up at the left margin setting.

A first line indent shifts the first line of a paragraph to the left by one tab stop. The remainder of the paragraph stays in its original location at the left margin setting.

On the other hand, a hanging indent will leave the first line of a paragraph in its original location at the left margin setting and indent the rest of the paragraph to the left by one tab stop.

Page 1   Sec 1   1/1   At 2.1"   Ln 8   Col 86   3:07 PM   REC MRK EXT OVR WPH

TIP

Fast Indent   To indent text quickly by one tab stop, use the **Indent** button from the Standard toolbar.

To undo an indent, use the **Decrease Indent** button from the Standard toolbar.

Formatting Your Document

INDENTING TEXT

Indenting Text

1 Place the cursor where text is to be indented, or select the text to be indented.

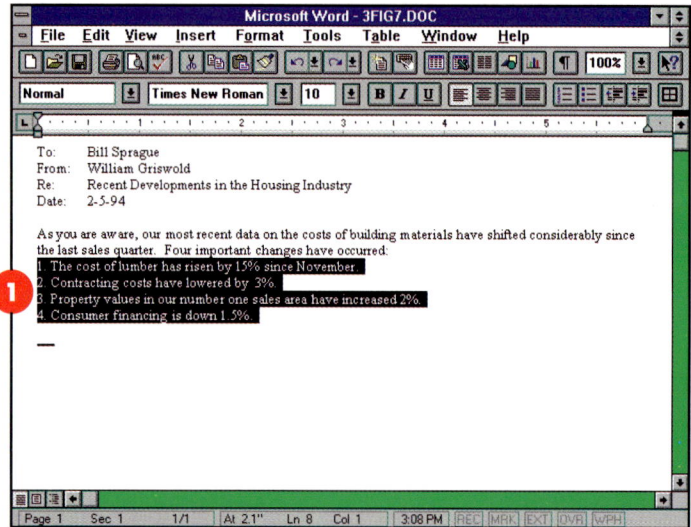

2 Click on **F**ormat or press **Alt+O**.

3 Click on **P**aragraph or press **P**.

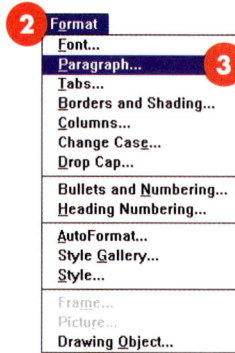

4 Choose an indent, or specify an indent in inches.

5 Click on **OK** or press **Enter**.

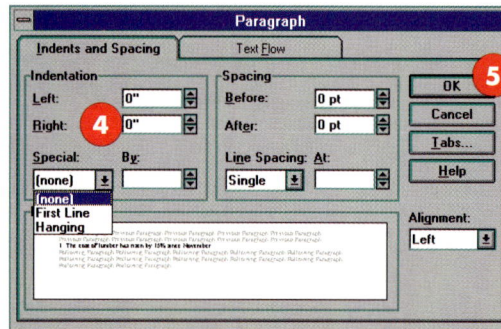

LEARNING THE LINGO

Indent: To shift text away from the margins.

TIP

Using Bulleted and Numbered Lists   Another form of indents are bulleted and numbered lists. These lists are common requirements for many types of documents.

A bulleted list is a list with a symbol to mark each paragraph. A numbered list is a list with sequentially-numbered paragraphs. You can quickly turn a series of paragraphs into either a bulleted or numbered list with these steps:

1. Select the paragraph(s) that you want to convert into a list.

2. Click on the **Number** or **Bullet** list button on the Formatting toolbar to create a numbered or bulleted list.

Number list

Bullet list

Formatting Your Document

ALIGNING TEXT

What Is Alignment?

Alignment, or *justification*, refers to the way text is positioned between the left and right margins in your Word for Windows document. Alignment means that the edges of your text line up. Word for Windows aligns text to the left automatically when you open a document. However, text can also be aligned to the right, centered between both margins, or fully justified—aligned at both the left and right margins.

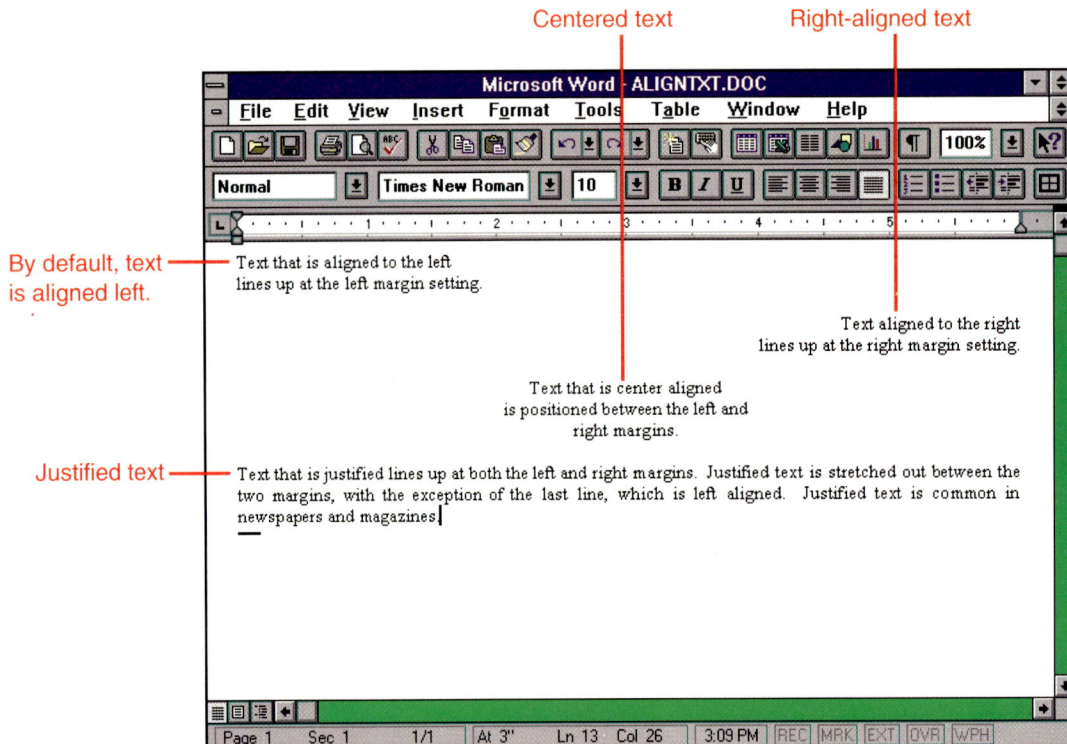

Centered text   Right-aligned text

Microsoft Word - ALIGNTXT.DOC

File   Edit   View   Insert   Format   Tools   Table   Window   Help

Normal   Times New Roman   10   B *I* U

By default, text is aligned left.

Text that is aligned to the left
lines up at the left margin setting.

Text aligned to the right
lines up at the right margin setting.

Text that is center aligned
is positioned between the left and
right margins.

Justified text

Text that is justified lines up at both the left and right margins. Justified text is stretched out between the two margins, with the exception of the last line, which is left aligned. Justified text is common in newspapers and magazines.

Page 1   Sec 1   1/1   At 3"   Ln 13   Col 26   3:09 PM   REC MRK EXT OVR WPH

LEARNING THE LINGO

Alignment: The positioning of text within a document in regard to the left and right margins. Also called justification.

TIP

Quick Align   To select a text alignment quickly, use the alignment buttons on the Formatting toolbar.

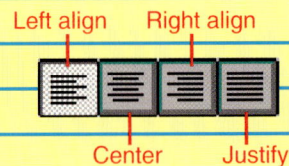

Left align   Right align

Center   Justify

Aligning Text

1 Position the cursor where text is to be entered, or select the text to be aligned.

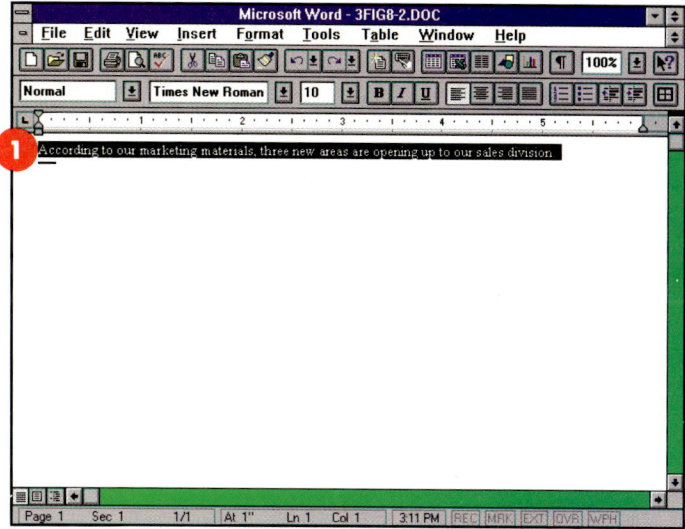

2 Click on Format or press **Alt+O**.

3 Click on **Paragraph** or press **P**.

4 Select the type of alignment to apply from the drop-down list in the Indents and Spacing tab.

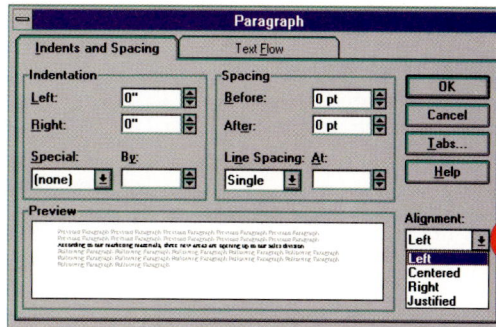

ALIGNING TEXT

Exercise

Type in the text block shown in the figure, and follow these steps to practice aligning.

1 Select the text block.

2 Click on **F**ormat or press **Alt+O**.

3 Click on **P**aragraph or press **P**.

4 Select the Alignment drop-down list on the **I**ndents and Spacing tab.

5 Click on **J**ustified or press **J**.

6 Click on **OK** or press **Enter**.

7 Repeat steps 1–6 using another type of alignment.

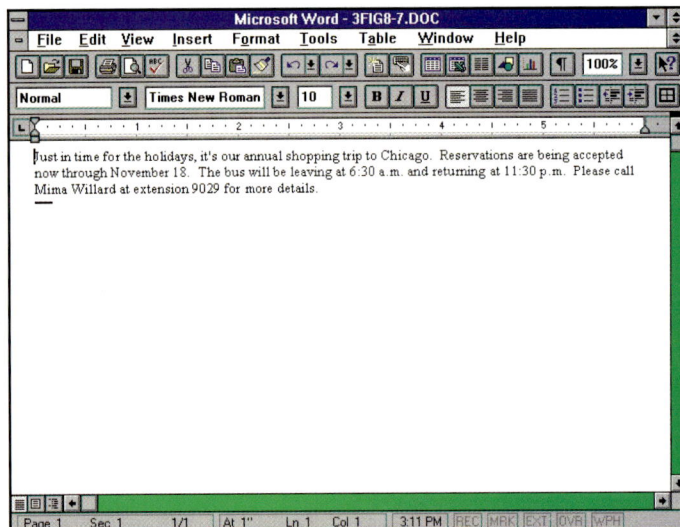

TIP

Vertical Alignment   Along with indents and alignment, you can also control the vertical positioning of your document. The **V**ertical Alignment command controls how the text in your document is spaced vertically, just as horizontal alignment controls how text is positioned horizontally.

You'll find the **V**ertical Alignment drop-down list in the **F**ile menu's Page Set**u**p dialog box.

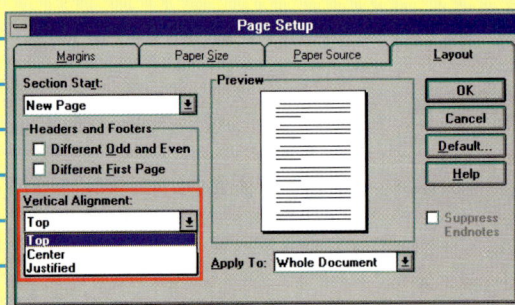

PART 4

Beyond the Basics

In this section you will learn some of Word's more advanced features. These features can help you work more accurately and efficiently toward the creation of impressive professional documents.

- Changing the Document Display Mode
- Working with Templates
- Creating a Template
- Working with Styles
- Creating a Style
- Using the Spell Checker
- Using the Thesaurus
- Using the Grammar Checker

CHANGING THE DOCUMENT DISPLAY MODE

What Is the Document Display Mode?

The document display mode determines how your document is displayed on the screen. Each mode is suitable for certain types of editing and writing tasks. There are three basic display modes to use: Normal, **Outline**, and **Page** Layout. These display modes are found on the **View** menu. When the **View** menu is pulled-down, you'll find a bullet displayed next to the view mode currently in effect.

In Normal mode, all text formatting (fonts, underline, and so on) is displayed, but the page layout is simplified to make typing and editing easier. **Normal** mode is suitable for most of your daily work.

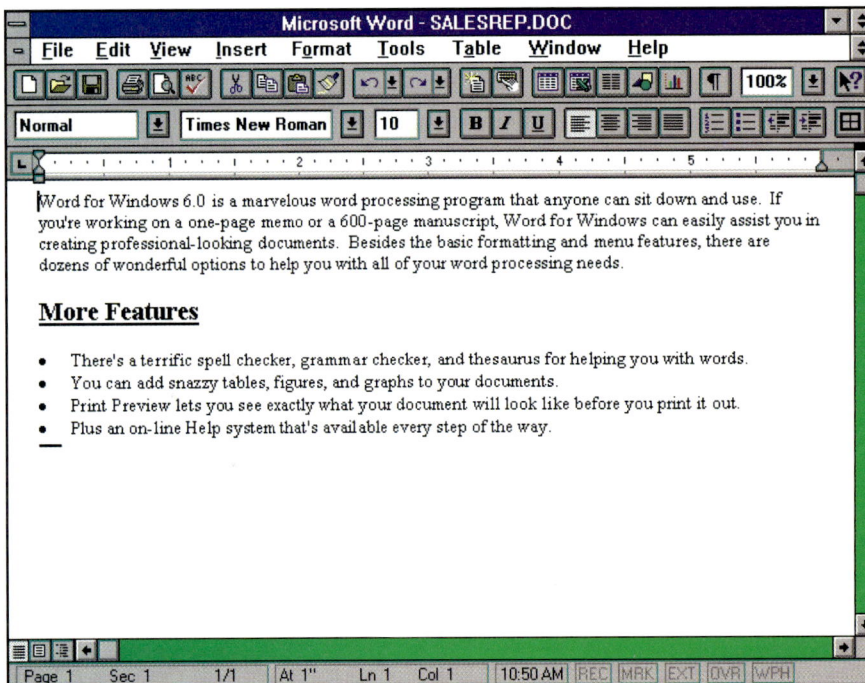

In **Outline** mode, text is displayed organized by style headings. **Outline** mode is suitable for creating outlines and for viewing the organization of a document. (See the task "Working With Styles" to learn more about style headings.)

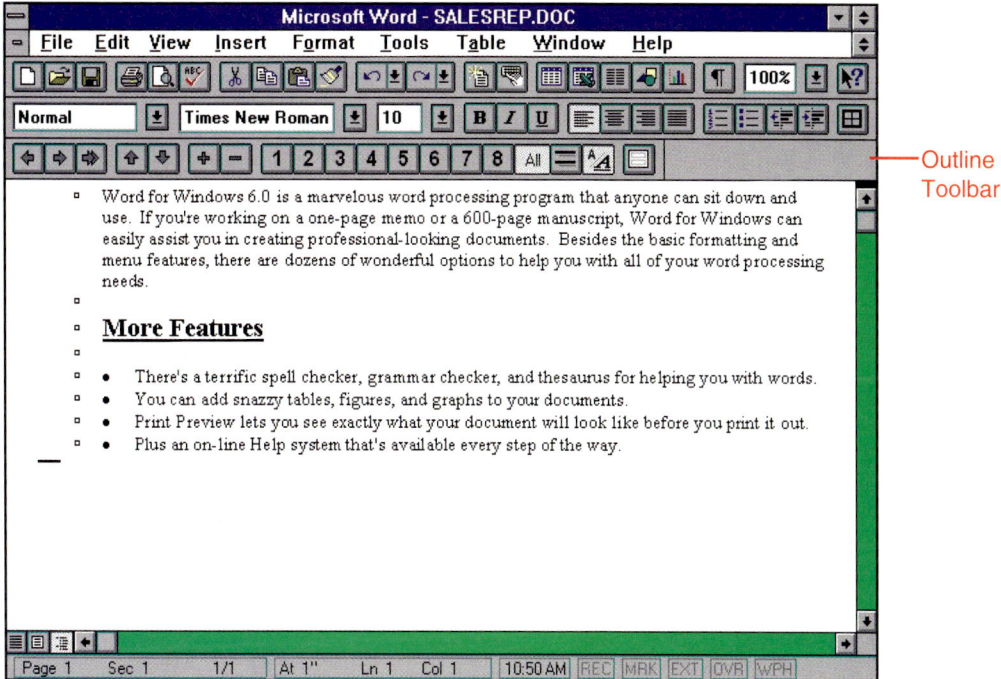

Outline
Toolbar

When you use **P**age Layout mode, text is displayed exactly as it will be printed. **P**age Layout mode is suitable for fine-tuning the appearance of your document. With **P**age Layout mode, a vertical ruler appears on the left side of your screen.

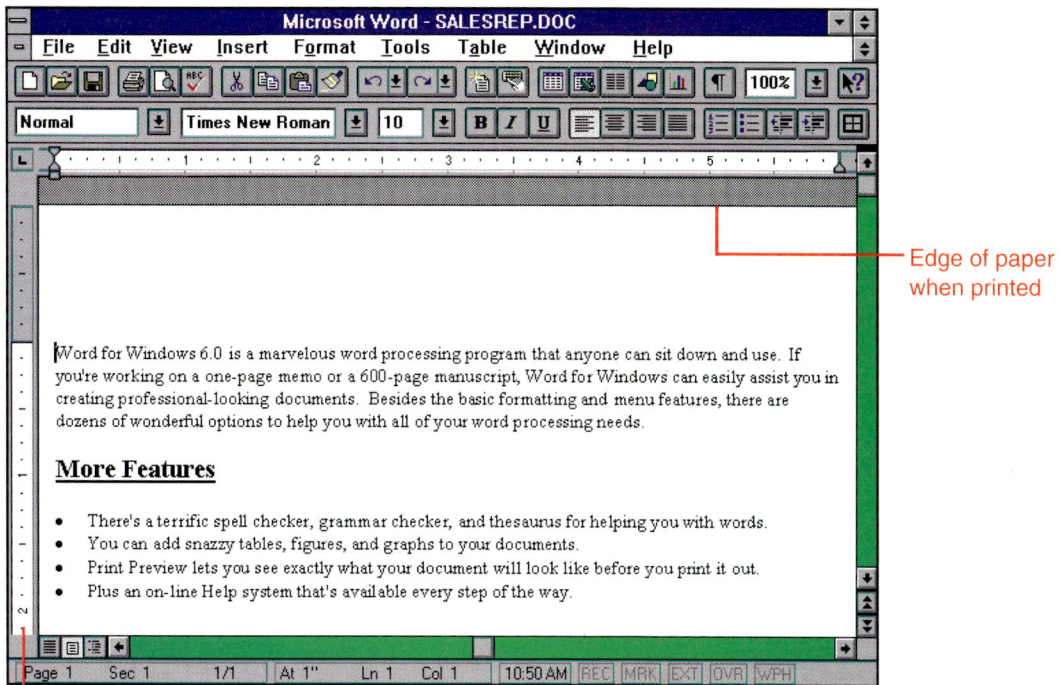

Edge of paper
when printed

A vertical ruler appears in Page Layout mode.

Beyond the Basics

Changing the Document Display Mode

1 Click on **View** or press **Alt+V**.

2 Click on **Normal** or press **N** for Normal mode. Click **Outline** or press **O** for Outline mode. Click **Page** Layout or press **P** for Page Layout mode.

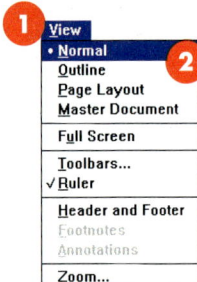

1 View
• **Normal**
2
Outline
Page Layout
Master Document

Full Screen

Toolbars...
√ Ruler

Header and Footer
Footnotes
Annotations

Zoom...

TIP

Outline Mode Tip   To use Outline mode, you must assign Word's predefined heading styles (Heading 1, Heading 2, and so on) to your document's headings. Paragraphs assigned the Heading 1 style become the top level heads in Outline Mode, and so on. For more information on assigning the heading styles, see the task "Working with Styles."

WORKING WITH TEMPLATES

What Is a Template?

A template is a model, or pattern, on which you base a document. A template can contain text and graphics that are the same for each document that's based on that template—your company letterhead, for example, or the standard elements of a FAX form. A template can also contain formatting, styles, and macros.

You must select a template when you start each new document. Word provides a number of predefined templates that you can use as-is or modify to suit your needs. You can also create your own templates from scratch. (See the task "Creating a Template" later in this section.)

To open a template, use the **New** command found on the **File** menu. The New dialog box will be displayed with a list of templates from which to choose.

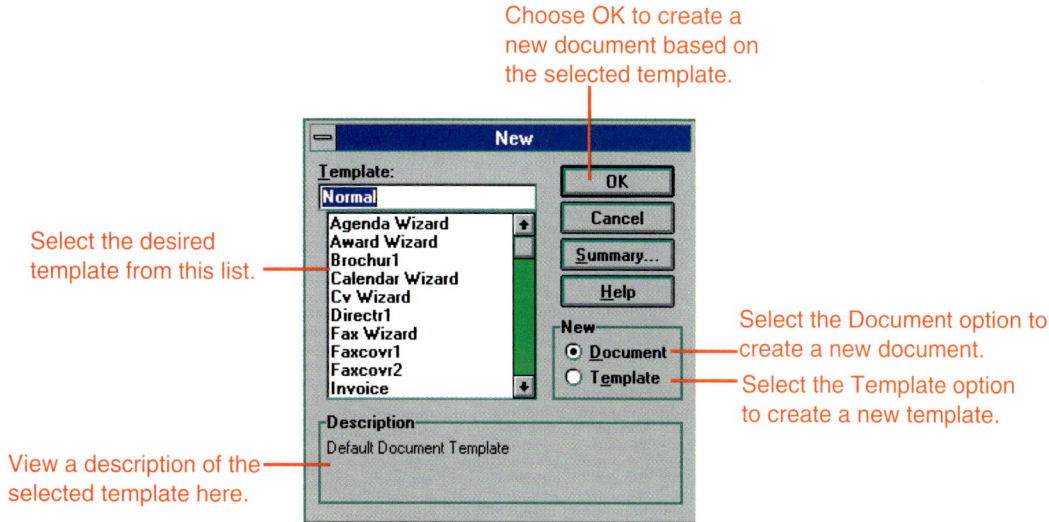

Choose OK to create a new document based on the selected template.

Select the desired template from this list.

View a description of the selected template here.

Select the Document option to create a new document.

Select the Template option to create a new template.

LEARNING THE LINGO

Style: A collection of specifications for formatting text (for example 12-point, centered Courier text). A style may include information for the font, size, style, margins, and spacing. Applying a style to text automatically formats the text according to that style's specifications.

Macro: A group of commands to execute, bundled together under one name. Rather than running each command separately, you just run the macro, and it in turn runs all the commands automatically.

Beyond the Basics

97

WORKING WITH TEMPLATES

To Start a Document Based on a Template

1 Click on **File** or press **Alt+F**.

2 Click on **New** or press **N**.

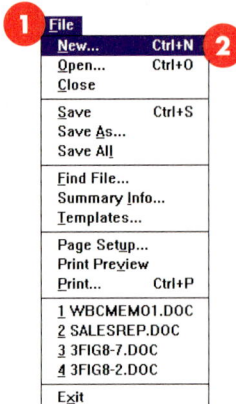

3 Select the desired template from the list.

4 Be sure that the Document option is selected by clicking on **Document** or pressing **Alt+D**.

5 Click on **OK** or press **Enter**.

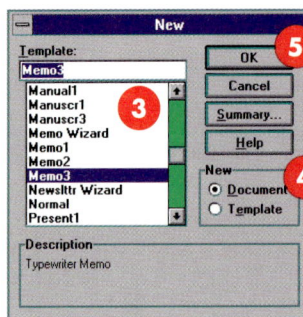

TIP

Which Template Do I Use? If you're not sure which template to use, select **Normal**. This is one of Word's predefined templates. It is a basic, blank template that is suitable for most documents.

TIP

Toolbar Shortcut To start a new document based on the Normal template, click on the **New document** tool on the Standard toolbar.

CREATING A TEMPLATE

When Should You Create Your Own Templates?

If you create multiple documents that have a similar format, creating and using a template for those documents can save you a lot of time. Good candidates for a template would be a FAX cover sheet, a memo form, or a purchase requisition. With a template for documents such as these, you only need to type the parts that are different each time you create a new document.

Creating a template is no different than creating a document. You insert the text and graphics, and define the formatting and styles that you want in all documents based on the new template. Word saves templates with a name you assign and the .DOT extension.

These are the elements that are part of the template.

These are the elements you add for each individual document.

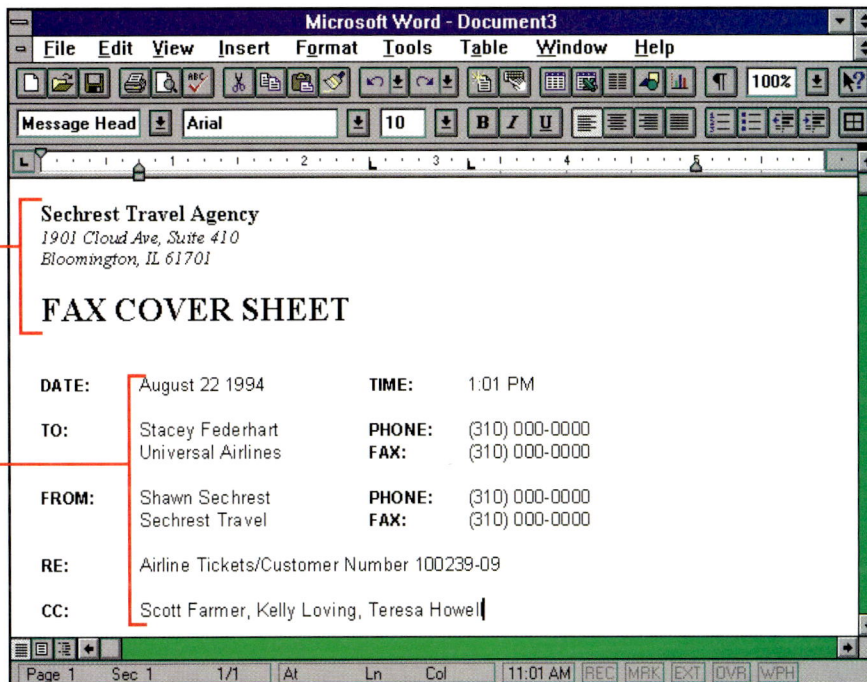

Microsoft Word - Document3

File Edit View Insert Format Tools Table Window Help

Message Head | Arial | 10 | B I U

Sechrest Travel Agency
1901 Cloud Ave, Suite 410
Bloomington, IL 61701

FAX COVER SHEET

DATE:	August 22 1994	**TIME:**	1:01 PM
TO:	Stacey Federhart	**PHONE:**	(310) 000-0000
	Universal Airlines	**FAX:**	(310) 000-0000
FROM:	Shawn Sechrest	**PHONE:**	(310) 000-0000
	Sechrest Travel	**FAX:**	(310) 000-0000
RE:	Airline Tickets/Customer Number 100239-09		
CC:	Scott Farmer, Kelly Loving, Teresa Howell		

Page 1 Sec 1 1/1 At Ln Col 11:01 AM REC MRK EXT OVR WPH

TIP

What Do I Base My Template On? If you're not sure which existing template to base your new template on, select **Normal**.

CREATING A TEMPLATE

How to Create a New Template

1 Click on **F**ile or press **Alt+F**.

2 Click on **N**ew or press **N**.

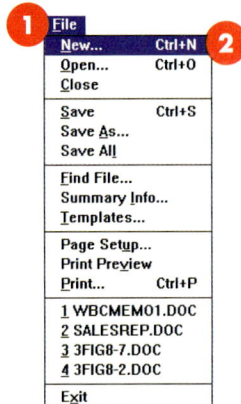

3 Select the Template option by clicking on T**e**mplate or pressing **Alt+E**.

4 From the **T**emplate list, select the existing template on which you want to base the new template.

5 Click on **OK** or press **Enter**.

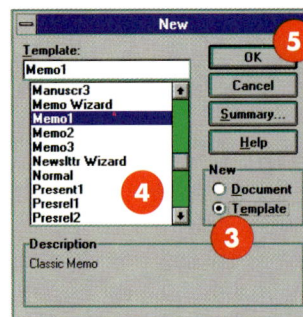

6 Enter the text, formatting, and styles that you want in the template.

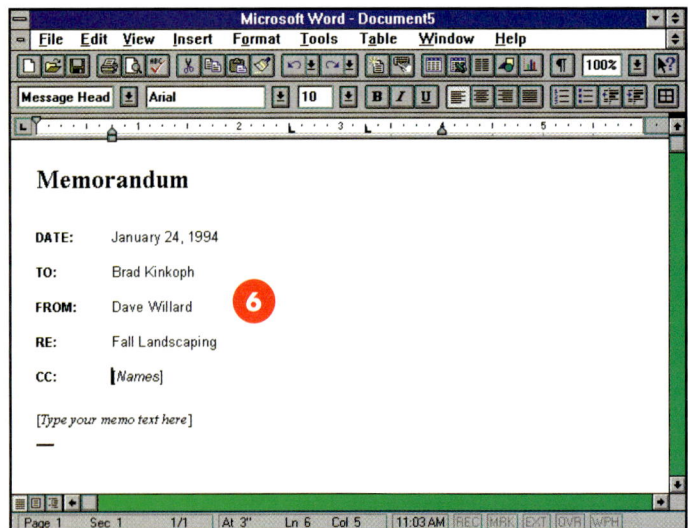

7 Click on **File** or press **Alt+F**.

8 Click on Save **As** or press **A**.

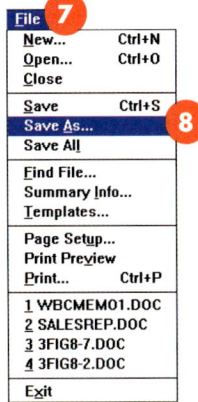

```
File                    7
  New...        Ctrl+N
  Open...       Ctrl+O
  Close
  Save          Ctrl+S
  Save As...            8
  Save All
  Find File...
  Summary Info...
  Templates...
  Page Setup...
  Print Preview
  Print...      Ctrl+P
  1 WBCMEMO1.DOC
  2 SALESREP.DOC
  3 3FIG8-7.DOC
  4 3FIG8-2.DOC
  Exit
```

9 Enter a 1–8 character name for the template.

10 Click on **OK** or press **Enter**.

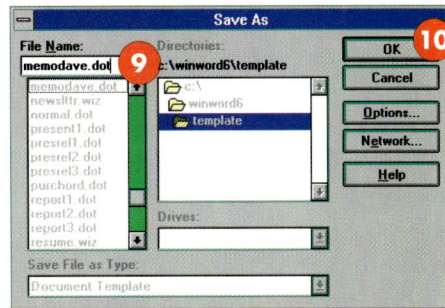

```
                    Save As
File Name:          Directories:          OK      10
memodave.dot        c:\winword6\template
memodave.dot          c:\                 Cancel
newsltr.wiz           winword6
normal.dot            template            Options...
present1.dot
presrel1.dot                              Network...
presrel2.dot
presrel3.dot                              Help
purchord.dot
report1.dot
report2.dot
report3.dot         Drives:
resume.wiz
Save File as Type:
Document Template
```

TIP

Modifying an Existing Template   You can easily modify an existing template to meet your needs.

Click on **F**ile, or press **Alt+F**. Then click on **O**pen, or press **O**. This will reveal the Open dialog box.

Select the name of the template you want to modify. Open the document and make your changes.

When you are finished, save the template.

Beyond the Basics

WORKING WITH STYLES

What Is a Style?

A style is a collection of formatting that has been assigned a name. A style can specify a certain font, line spacing, and indentation. For example, if you use a bold, centered, 24-point Courier heading in many reports, you could create a style called BOLDHEAD and then apply the style to each paragraph that you wanted to appear that way.

By assigning a style to a paragraph, you automatically apply all of the style's formatting to that paragraph. If you later go back and modify the style's formatting, the new formatting will automatically be applied to all paragraphs in the document with that style.

Word has a number of predefined styles, and you can also create your own. The default style is Normal.

How to Assign a Style to a Paragraph

1 Move the cursor anywhere in the paragraph. Or to assign to multiple paragraphs, select the paragraphs.

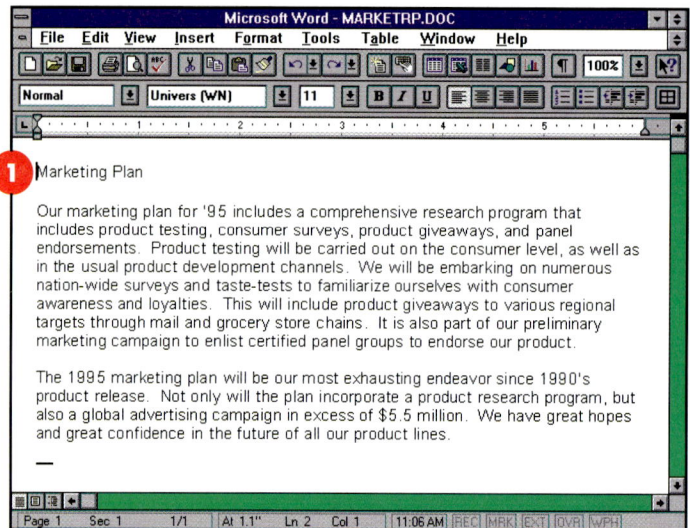

2 Click the down arrow next to the Style box on the Formatting toolbar.

3 Click the name of the style you want.

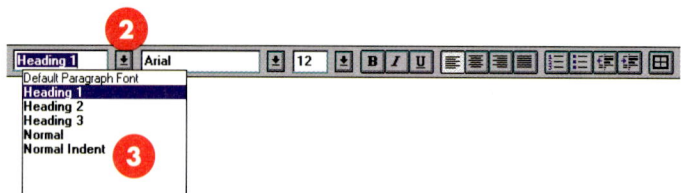

Exercise

Enter the text shown in the figure and practice assigning styles to the paragraphs.

1 Assign the style "Heading 1" to the first line.

2 Assign the style "Heading 2" to the second line.

3 Assign the style "Normal" to the paragraph below the first two lines.

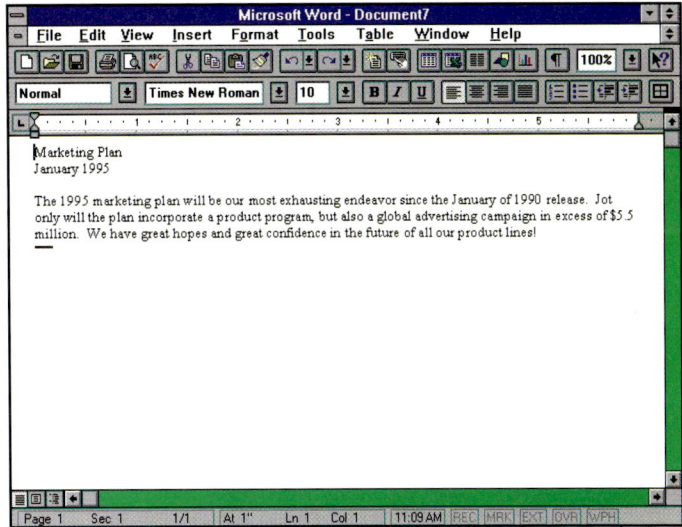

```
Microsoft Word - Document7
File   Edit   View   Insert   Format   Tools   Table   Window   Help

Normal      Times New Roman    10    B  I  U

Marketing Plan
January 1995

The 1995 marketing plan will be our most exhausting endeavor since the January of 1990 release.  Jot
only will the plan incorporate a product program, but also a global advertising campaign in excess of $5.5
million.  We have great hopes and great confidence in the future of all our product lines!

Page 1   Sec 1        1/1     At 1"    Ln 1   Col 1      11:09 AM  REC  MRK  EXT  OVR  WPH
```

TIP

Style Tips   Word's predefined styles include several useful formats that you can use or modify to suit your needs.

The Style box on the Formatting toolbar displays the name of the style assigned to the paragraph containing the cursor.

QUICK REFRESHER

Selecting Paragraphs

To select one paragraph, double-click in the selection bar to the left of the paragraph.

To select multiple paragraphs, click next to the first line of the first paragraph in the selection bar, and then drag to the last line of the last paragraph.

Beyond the Basics

CREATING A STYLE

Why Create Styles?

You are not limited to the styles that come with Word; you can create your own. When you create a style, you assign a single name to a group of formatting attributes — for example, FOOTNOTE style might be 10-point Arial italic with a hanging indent. Then when you need a paragraph to be formatted in that style, you simply apply the style, rather than applying each attribute separately.

To create a style, apply the desired formatting to a paragraph. With the cursor in that paragraph, use the **S**tyle command found on the F**o**rmat menu to display the Style dialog box. Then click on the **N**ew button or press **N** to access the New Style dialog box to assign a name.

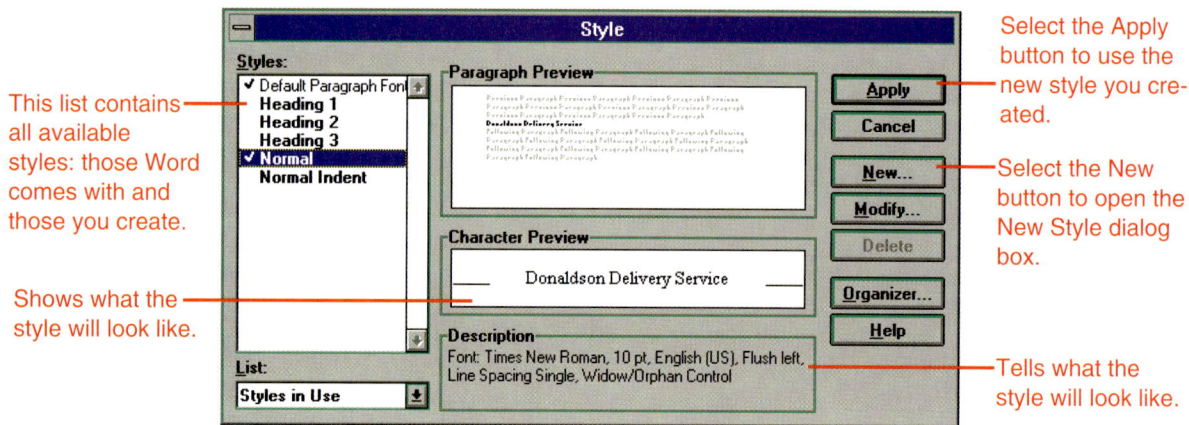

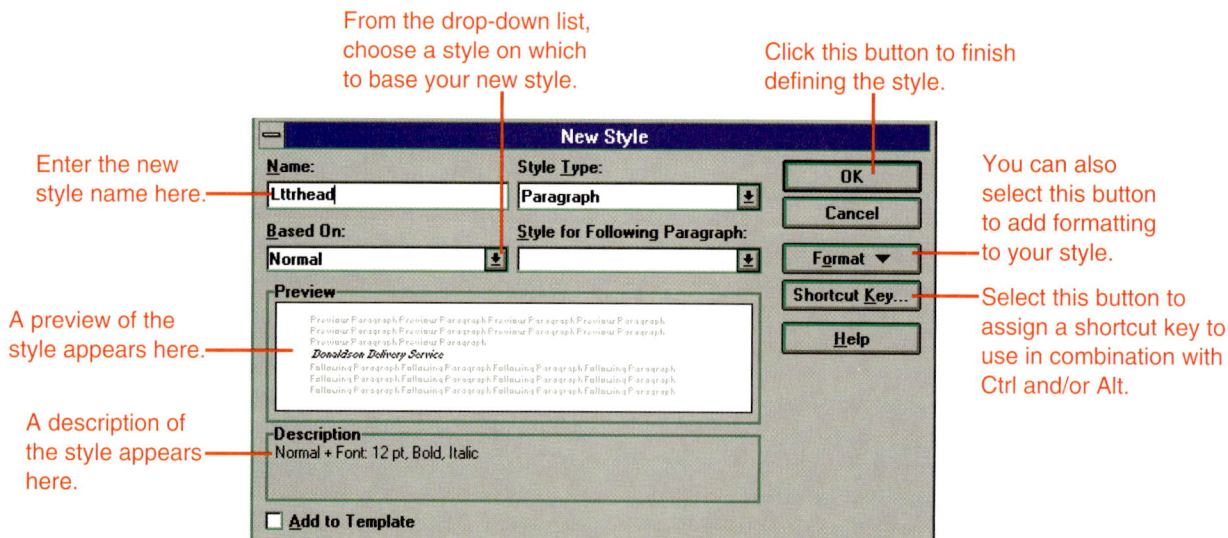

This list contains all available styles: those Word comes with and those you create.

Shows what the style will look like.

Select the Apply button to use the new style you created.

Select the New button to open the New Style dialog box.

Tells what the style will look like.

From the drop-down list, choose a style on which to base your new style.

Click this button to finish defining the style.

Enter the new style name here.

You can also select this button to add formatting to your style.

A preview of the style appears here.

Select this button to assign a shortcut key to use in combination with Ctrl and/or Alt.

A description of the style appears here.

How to Create a Style

1 Format a paragraph with the formatting that you want in the new style. Be sure the cursor is in the paragraph.

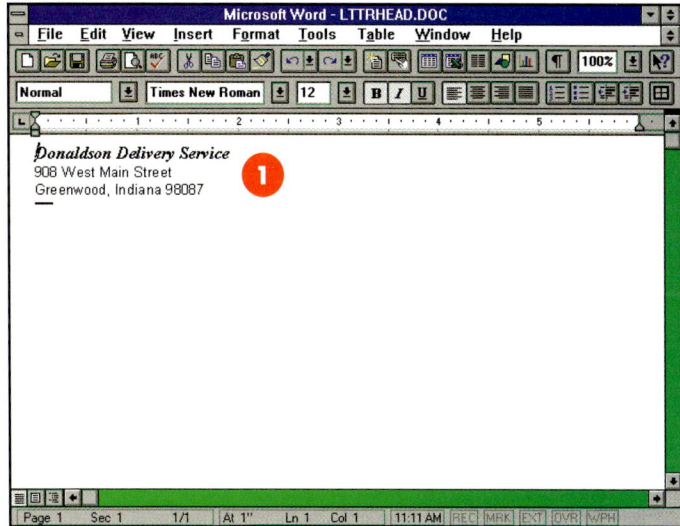

2 Click on Format or press **Alt+O**.

3 Click Style or press **S**.

4 Click on New or press **Alt+N** to display the New Style dialog box.

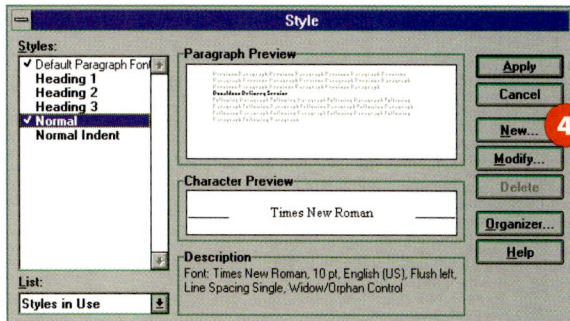

105

CREATING A STYLE

5 Enter the new style name in the **Name** box.

6 If you want to assign a shortcut key combination to the style, click on Shortcut **Key** or press **Alt+K**.

7 When you are finished selecting style options, click on **OK** or press **Enter**.

8 Click on the **Apply** button to save the new style, or press **Alt+A**.

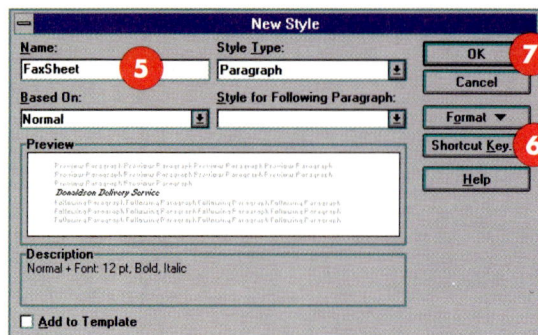

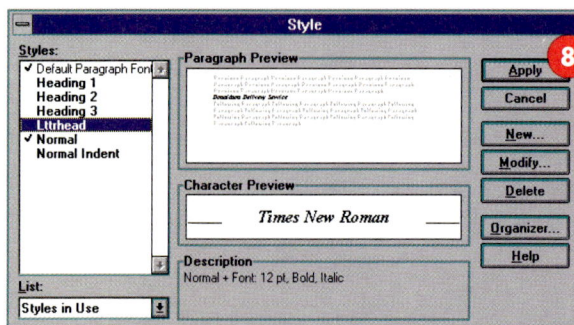

LEARNING THE LINGO

Shortcut Key: A key combination that you can press to quickly execute a command, apply a style, or perform some other action.

Exercise

Enter the paragraph shown in the figure. Format the paragraph and create a new style based on the formatting.

1 Indent the paragraph 0.5 inches from the left.

2 Select the entire paragraph and press **Ctrl+B** to bold it.

3 Select F**o**rmat **S**tyle to activate the Style box, and then click on **New** or press **Alt+N** to display the New Style dialog box.

4 Type **Bold Indent** and press **Enter**.

5 Click on the **A**pply button or press **Alt+A** to save the new style.

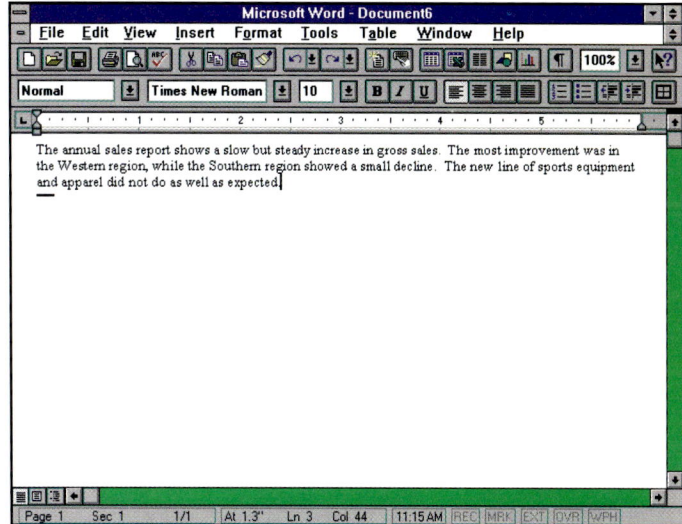

Microsoft Word - Document6

File Edit View Insert Format Tools Table Window Help

Normal | Times New Roman | 10 | B I U

The annual sales report shows a slow but steady increase in gross sales. The most improvement was in the Western region, while the Southern region showed a small decline. The new line of sports equipment and apparel did not do as well as expected.

Page 1   Sec 1   1/1   At 1.3"   Ln 3   Col 44   11:15 AM   REC MRK EXT OVR WPH

TIP

Editing an Existing Style   When you edit a style, you change the formatting commands that are associated with the style name. By editing a style you can quickly change the formatting of all the paragraphs in the document that have been assigned that style.

To edit a style, open the Style dialog box by clicking on F**o**rmat or pressing **Alt+O**, and then clicking **S**tyle or pressing **S**. In the Style dialog box, select the **M**odify button. Make any changes to the style using the F**o**rmat button to edit text or paragraph formatting.

Beyond the Basics

USING THE SPELL CHECKER

Why Check Your Spelling?

Even the best spellers make spelling errors, even if it's only a typographical error. Word's spelling checker can scan all or part of your document, reporting each word not found in its dictionary. You can ignore the word, add it to the dictionary, or use one of Word's suggested replacements.

To check a document's spelling use the **S**pelling command located in the **T**ools menu. When Word finds a word not in its dictionary, it highlights the word in the document and displays the Spelling dialog box.

A suggested replacement is listed here.

Replace the word with the suggested replacement. Ignore the word.

The misspelled word is displayed.

Select another replacement from this list.

Use this option to correct future misspellings of a word.

Ignore all occurrences of the word.

Replace all occurrences of the word in the document with the suggested replacement.

Spelling: English (US)

Not in Dictionary: tomatos

Change To: tomatoes
Suggestions:
tomatoes
tomato's
tomato

Add Words To: CUSTOM.DIC

AutoCorrect | Options... | Undo Last | Cancel | Help

Ignore | Ignore All
Change | Change All
Add | Suggest

Undo the last replacement.

Add the word to the dictionary.

TIP

Toolbar Shortcut   You can start a spelling check by clicking on the

Spelling tool on the Standard toolbar. To check the spelling of a

single word, select the word and then click on the **Spelling** tool.

ABC
✓

Checking Spelling

1 Move the cursor to the beginning of the document by pressing **Ctrl+Home**.

CTRL + HOME

2 Click on Tools or press **Alt+T**.

3 Click on Spelling or press **S**.

```
Tools
Spelling...          F7
Grammar...
Thesaurus...    Shift+F7
Hyphenation...
Language...
Word Count...

Mail Merge...
Envelopes and Labels...

Protect Document...
Revisions...

Macro...
Customize...
Options...
```

4 Each word not found in the dictionary is displayed.

5 Enter a replacement word, or select it from the list.

6 Click Ignore or Ignore All or press **Alt+I** or **Alt+G** to ignore one or all occurrences of the word.

7 Click on Add or press **Alt+A** to add the word to the dictionary.

8 Click Change or Change All or press **Alt+C** or **Alt+L** to replace one or all occurrences of the word with the suggested replacement.

9 Click Undo Last or press **Alt+U** to undo the last replacement.

10 Click **Cancel** to end the spelling check operation, or press **Esc**.

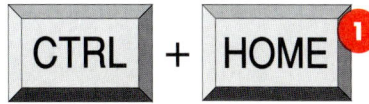

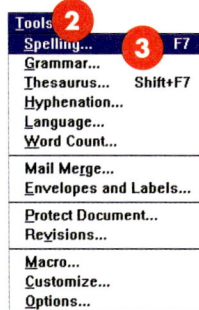

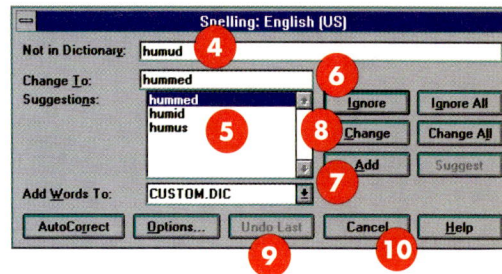

Spelling: English (US)
Not in Dictionary: humud
Change To: hummed
Suggestions: hummed / humid / humus
Ignore / Ignore All / Change / Change All / Add / Suggest
Add Words To: CUSTOM.DIC
AutoCorrect / Options... / Undo Last / Cancel / Help

Beyond the Basics

USING THE THESAURUS

What Is a Thesaurus?

A thesaurus is used to look up synonyms for words, that is, words that have the same or a similar meaning. You can use Word's thesaurus to add variety to your writing and to help you find the best word to use in a particular situation.

To use the thesaurus, position the cursor in or just to the left of the word you want to look up, and then issue the **T**hesaurus command from the **T**ools menu. This command displays the Thesaurus dialog box.

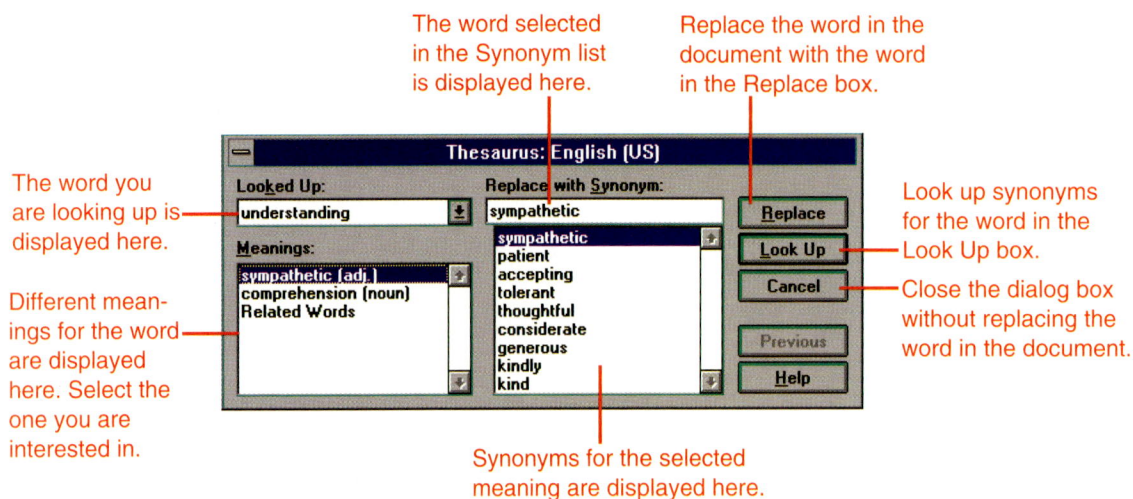

The word selected in the Synonym list is displayed here.

Replace the word in the document with the word in the Replace box.

The word you are looking up is displayed here.

Thesaurus: English (US)

Looked Up:
understanding

Replace with Synonym:
sympathetic

Meanings:
sympathetic (adj.)
comprehension (noun)
Related Words

sympathetic
patient
accepting
tolerant
thoughtful
considerate
generous
kindly
kind

Replace
Look Up
Cancel
Previous
Help

Look up synonyms for the word in the Look Up box.

Close the dialog box without replacing the word in the document.

Different meanings for the word are displayed here. Select the one you are interested in.

Synonyms for the selected meaning are displayed here.

TIP

Thesaurus Shortcut   You can quickly display the Thesaurus dialog box by pressing **Shift+F7**.

Using the Thesaurus

1 Position the cursor in or next to the word of interest in the document.

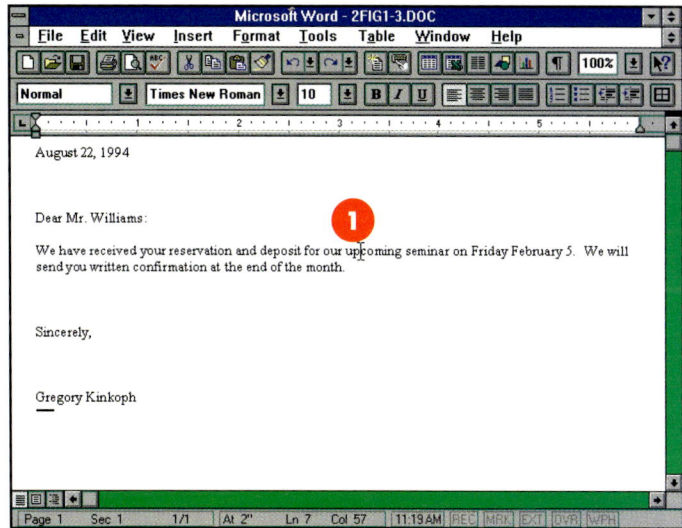

2 Click on **Tools** or press **Alt+T**.

3 Click on **Thesaurus** or press **T**.

4 Select the proper meaning of the word.

5 Select the desired synonym.

6 Click **R**eplace or press **Enter**.

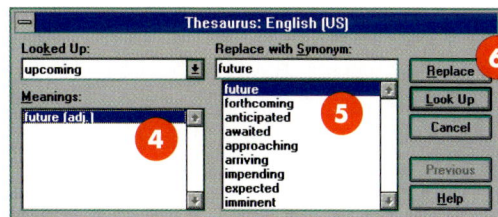

Beyond the Basics

USING THE GRAMMAR CHECKER

Why Check Your Grammar?

In the "Using the Spell Checker" task earlier in this section, you learned how to make Word for Windows 6.0 proofread your documents for spelling errors. But spelling errors aren't the only errors that occur in documents. Grammatical errors are also a problem—and the spell-checking tool doesn't look for grammatical errors, just spelling errors.

Thankfully, Word for Windows also comes with a grammar checker. The grammar checker searches your entire document for mistakes in grammar.

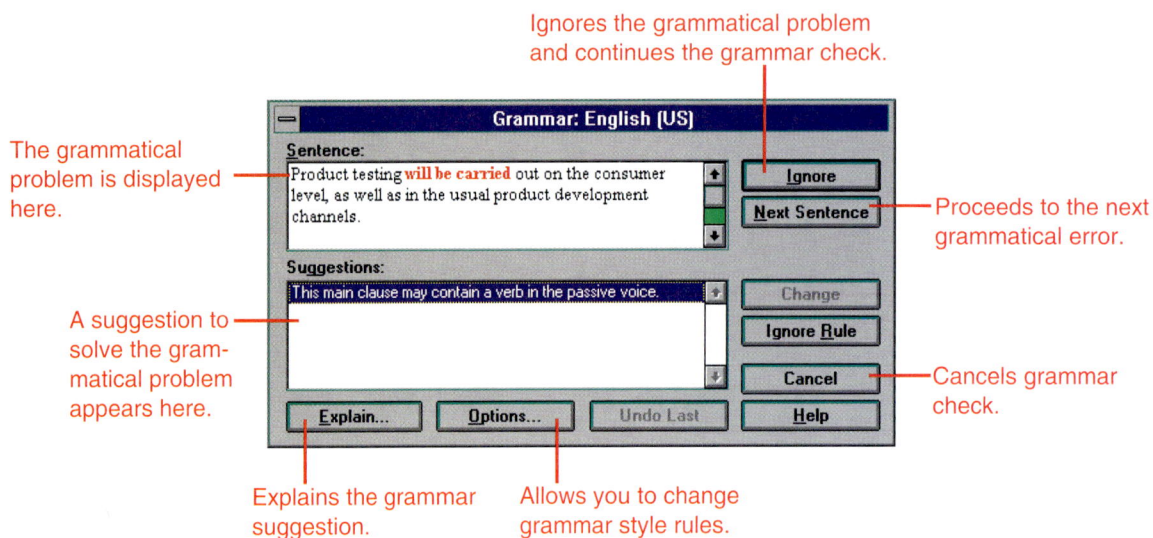

Ignores the grammatical problem and continues the grammar check.

The grammatical problem is displayed here.

Grammar: English (US)

Sentence:
Product testing **will be carried** out on the consumer level, as well as in the usual product development channels.

Proceeds to the next grammatical error.

A suggestion to solve the grammatical problem appears here.

Suggestions:
This main clause may contain a verb in the passive voice.

Ignore

Next Sentence

Change

Ignore Rule

Cancel

Explain...

Options...

Undo Last

Help

Cancels grammar check.

Explains the grammar suggestion.

Allows you to change grammar style rules.

Checking Your Grammar

1 Move the cursor to the beginning of the document by pressing **Ctrl+Home**.

2 Click on **T**ools or press **Alt+T**.

3 Click on **G**rammar or press **G**.

4 If a problem is found, a message appears in the message box.

5 Choose from the option buttons to address the problem and continue the grammar check.

6 When the grammar check is complete, a dialog box will appear revealing the Readability Statistics box. Click **OK** or press **Enter**.

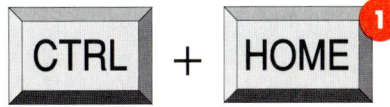

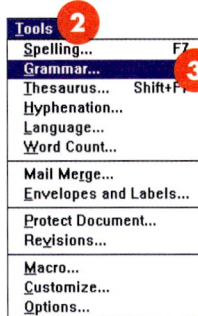

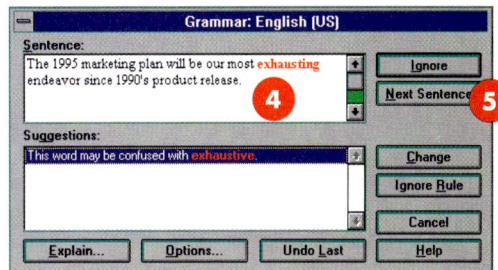

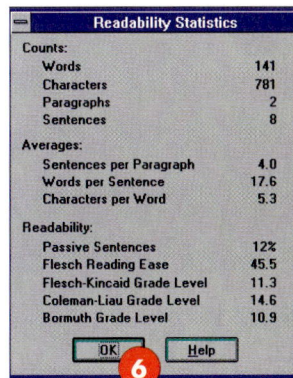

CTRL + HOME

Tools
Spelling...   F7
Grammar...
Thesaurus...   Shift+F7
Hyphenation...
Language...
Word Count...

Mail Merge...
Envelopes and Labels...

Protect Document...
Revisions...

Macro...
Customize...
Options...

Grammar: English (US)

Sentence:
The 1995 marketing plan will be our most exhausting endeavor since 1990's product release.

Ignore
Next Sentence

Suggestions:
This word may be confused with exhaustive.

Change
Ignore Rule
Cancel
Help

Explain...   Options...   Undo Last

Readability Statistics

Counts:
Words	141
Characters	781
Paragraphs	2
Sentences	8

Averages:
Sentences per Paragraph	4.0
Words per Sentence	17.6
Characters per Word	5.3

Readability:
Passive Sentences	12%
Flesch Reading Ease	45.5
Flesch-Kincaid Grade Level	11.3
Coleman-Liau Grade Level	14.6
Bormuth Grade Level	10.9

OK   Help

Beyond the Basics

Glossary

active document   The document you are currently working on. It will have a highlighted title bar. When more than one document is opened, only one window can be worked on at a time.

alignment   Positioning of text between the left and right margins. Also known as *justification*.

attributes   Changes made in the look of text, such as making it bolder and larger, or changing its positioning. Also called *formatting*.

click   To tap or press the left mouse button.

Clipboard   A temporary storage area built into most Windows-based programs. You can put a selection into the Clipboard with the Cut or Copy commands, and retrieve a selection from the Clipboard with the Paste command.

cursor   A blinking vertical line that indicates where typed characters will appear. Also known as the *insertion point*.

directory   Special areas in your computer's hard disk where files are stored.

disk drive   A device that writes data to a magnetic disk and reads data from the disk.

document   Work, such as a letter or a memo, created using a word processing program.

DOS prompt   A set of characters (usually **C:\>**) on the left side of the screen, followed by a blinking underline. DOS commands are typed in at the DOS prompt.

double-click   To tap the mouse button twice in rapid succession.

drag   To press and hold the mouse button while moving the mouse to a new location.

file name   A name assigned to a document stored on disk. You designate the first part of the name, up to 8 characters. Word automatically adds the extension ".DOC" at the end of the file name.

floppy disk   A small, portable magnetic disk used to save and store the data created on your computer.

font   A set of characters with a specific design.

hanging indent   An indent with the first line of the text block flush left with the left margin, and the remainder of the text block indented. Hanging indents are typically used with bulleted or numbered lists.

hard disk   A permanent disk drive located inside your computer. Hard disks hold more data than floppy disks.

I-beam   The "Capital I" shape the mouse pointer assumes when it is anywhere inside the text area of your screen.

icon   A small picture on-screen that represents a program, an action you can take, or a piece of information.

GLOSSARY

Insert mode   Adding text without deleting any existing characters. Existing text is shifted to the right of the insertion point as new text is typed.

landscape orientation   Lines of text are parallel to the paper's long edge.

leader character   A character, such as a hyphen, that fills the tab space between words.

macro   A group of commands to execute, bundled together under one name. Rather than running each command separately, you just run the macro, and it in turn runs all the commands automatically.

margin   The space between your text and the outer edge of your page.

mouse   A device used to move the cursor or the highlighting around the computer screen to point at various program elements and to select them.

Overstrike mode   Adding text that takes the place of existing text. Also called *typeover mode*.

point   A measurement of character size and spacing. There are 72 points in an inch.

portrait orientation   Lines of text are parallel to the paper's short edge.

selection bar   The part of the screen to the left of the text. It can be used with the mouse to select text.

selection letter   An underlined letter in the menu or command name. Keyboard users can choose the command or menu by holding down the **Alt** key and pressing the underlined selection letter.

shortcut key   A key, or combination of keys, you can use to issue a command without using the menus.

style   A collection of specifications for formatting text (for example 12-point centered Courier text). A style may include information for the font, size, style, margins, and spacing. Applying a style to text automatically formats the text according to that style's specifications.

tab   A keystroke that moves text to a specified point in your document. Tabs are used to align text.

Thesaurus   A special program within WordPerfect for Windows 6.0 that allows you to look up synonyms and antonyms.

wrapping   Automatically starting a new line when you reach the right margin.

zoom   To magnify a portion of a document.

WORD FOR WINDOWS INSTALLATION

Before you can use Microsoft Word to create and edit documents, the program must be installed on your computer. The installation may have already been performed, in which case you are all set and can skip this section. If not, you will need to install the program.

You will need the diskettes that came with the Microsoft Word for Windows package. These are either 3 1/2- or 5 1/4-inch diskettes that are labeled Disk 1, Disk 2, and so on. Once you have located the diskettes, you are ready to begin.

1 If necessary, turn on your computer and start Windows by typing **win**.

2 Place installation disk number 1 in your computer's diskette drive.

3 From the Program Manager screen, click on **F**ile or press **Alt+F** to display the File menu.

4 Select **R**un from the **F**ile menu by clicking on **R**un or pressing **R**. This will display the Run dialog box.

5 In the Command Line text box type **a:setup** (if you placed the diskette in drive A:) or **b:setup** (if you placed the diskette in drive B:), and then press **Enter** or click **OK**.

Run
Command Line:	OK
b:setup	Cancel
☐ Run Minimized	Browse...
	Help

6 When prompted, enter your name and appropriate organization, and then choose a directory in which to install Word for Windows. The default directory is C:\WINWORD. Unless you have a specific reason to install Word in another directory, you should accept this by clicking Continue or pressing Enter.

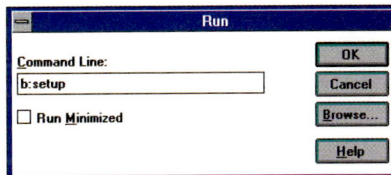

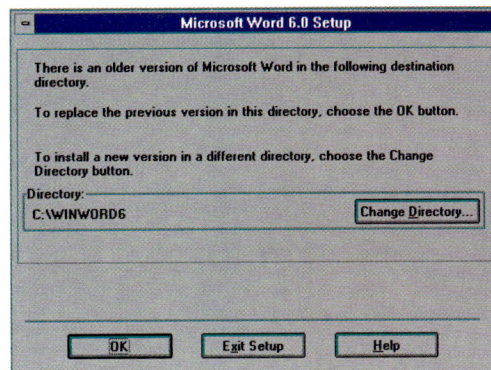

Microsoft Word 6.0 Setup
There is an older version of Microsoft Word in the following destination directory.
To replace the previous version in this directory, choose the OK button.
To install a new version in a different directory, choose the Change Directory button.
Directory:
C:\WINWORD6	Change Directory...
OK	Exit Setup	Help

117

7 Next, the Setup program gives you a choice of three installation options. Select **Typical** by clicking the corresponding button.

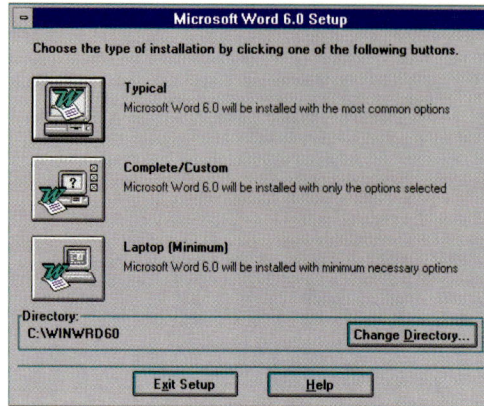

The Setup program will now begin copying the necessary files from the installation diskettes to your computer's hard disk. All you need to do is follow the instructions on-screen, changing diskettes when prompted.

When the installation is complete, you will return to the Program Manager screen. You are now ready to run Word!

Index

Index

Read Less & Learn Faster
with the Complete Line of
Show me
Visual Guides

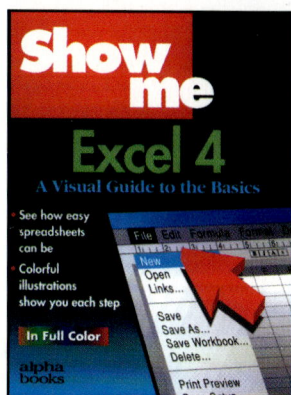

Show Me Excel 4
ISBN: 1-56761-179-6
Softbound, **$12.95 USA**

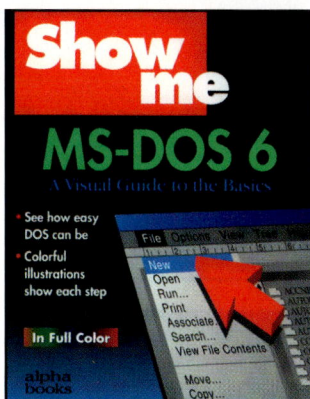

Show Me MS-DOS 6
ISBN: 1-56761-237-7
Softbound, **$12.95 USA**

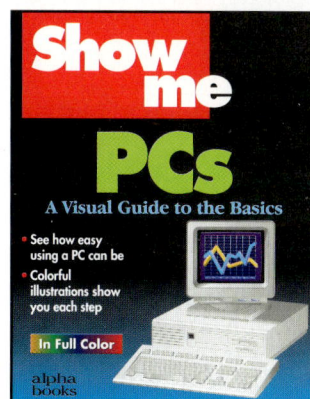

Show Me PCs
ISBN: 1-56761-260-1
Softbound, **$12.95 USA**

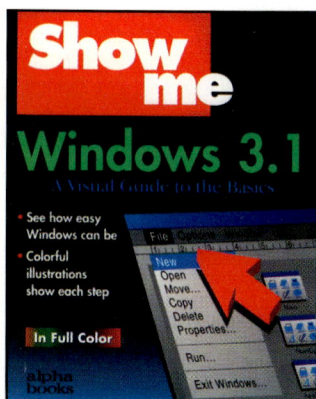

Show Me Windows 3.1
ISBN: 1-56761-236-9
Softbound, **$12.95 USA**

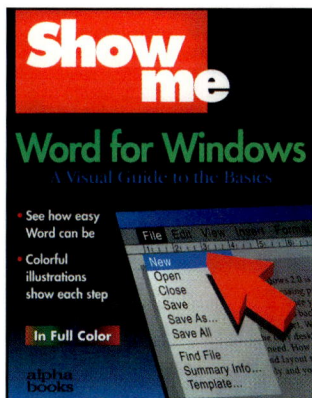

Show Me Word for Windows
ISBN: 1-56761-347-0
Softbound, **$12.95 USA**

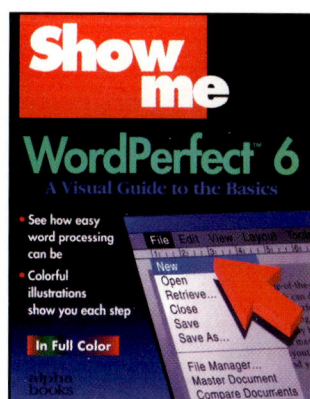

Show Me WordPerfect 6
ISBN: 1-56761-177-X
Softbound, **$12.95 USA**